Continuum Research Methods

Action Research

Continuum Research Methods Series

Series Editor: Richard Andrews

Real World Research Series

Series Editor: Bill Gillham

Action Research

Patrick J. M. Costello

continuum
LONDON • NEW YORK

Continuum

The Tower Building   15 East 26th Street
11 York Road   New York
London SE1 7NX   NY 10010
www.continuumbooks.com

First published 2003

British Library Cataloguing in Publication Data
A catalogue record for this book is available from the British Library.

ISBN 0 8264 6479 3

Library of Congress Cataloging-in-Publication Data
A catalogue record for this book has been applied for.

Typeset by Photoprint, Torquay, Devon
Printed and bound in Great Britain by MPG Books, Bodmin, Cornwall

Contents

Series Editor's Introduction

The *Continuum Research Methods* series aims to provide undergraduate, Masters and research students with accessible and authoritative guides to particular aspects of research methodology. Each title looks specifically at one topic and gives it in-depth treatment, very much in the tradition of the *Rediguide* series of the 1960s and 1970s.

Such an approach allows students to choose the books that are most appropriate to their own projects, whether they are working on a short dissertation, a medium-length work (15–40 000 words) or a fully-fledged thesis at MPhil or PhD level. Each title includes examples of students' work, clear explication of the principles and practices involved, and summaries of how best to check that your research is on course.

In due course, individual titles will be combined into larger books and, subsequently, into encyclopaedic works for reference.

The series will also be of use to researchers designing funded projects, and to supervisors who wish to recommend in-depth help to their research students.

Richard Andrews

Acknowledgements

I should like to thank the following:

Professor Richard Andrews for his kind invitation to contribute to this series.
Dr Donald Costello for the many discussions we have had about the action research cycle.
Christina Parkinson for her support and encouragement in the preparation of the volume.

Since 1986, I have had the opportunity to test and improve my thinking about many of the key ideas presented in this book. With this in mind, I am very grateful to those teachers and student teachers with whom I have worked, at the University of Hull, NEWI, and on behalf of the General Teaching Council for Wales, to develop a broad range of action research projects.
This book is for my son, Thomas Rónan Costello.

1

What is Action Research?

The central purposes of these pages are to enable action research practitioners to undertake and to offer an account of a project. Following are seven sections, the first six of which are headed by a commonly-asked question. Having examined the nature of action research and arguments for undertaking it in educational settings, I shall focus on developing an appropriate project, data collection and analysis, and producing a research report. The final section offers suggestions for further reading.

The nature of action research

In order to undertake an action research project within educational settings, we need to begin by giving some thought to the question: 'What is action research?' This, in turn, raises two further questions: 'What is research?' and 'What is educational research?' How are we to respond to these questions? One effective way of doing so is to place them in order, beginning with the most general, and then to do some reading and thinking about each in turn:

What is research?
What is educational research?
What is action research?

Of the three questions, the most general is: 'What is research?' As a starting point, it is useful to examine some texts that discuss a broad range of approaches to engaging in research. These reveal that there are: (1) many different types of research; and (2) numerous views as to the nature of each, how it should be conducted and what it aims to achieve.

For example, when discussing social research, Robson (2002, p. 26) cites the following: 'ethnography, quantitative behavioural science, phenomenology, action research, hermeneutics, evaluation research, feminist research, critical social science, historical-comparative research, and theoretical research'. It is useful to compare this list with some examples offered by Blaxter *et al.* (1996, p. 5): 'pure, applied and strategic research; descriptive, explanatory and evaluation research ... exploratory, testing-out and problem-solving research; covert, adversarial and collaborative research; basic, applied, instrumental and action research'.

When reading general texts, you will see many references to these (and other) kinds of research. At this stage, it is important to note several points. First of all, do not be confused or distracted by the 'labels' that are attached to various kinds of research. Instead, ask yourself:

1. What sorts of practices are being engaged in by those who undertake action research, ethnography, evaluation research etc.?
2. What rationale is offered to support these practices?

In looking for commonalities between the types of research they cite, Blaxter *et al.* (1996, p. 5) offer a succinct summary: 'the basic characteristics shared by all of these ... is that they are, or aim to be, planned, cautious, systematic and reliable ways of finding out or deepening understanding'.

Second, look for references to the particular kinds of research in which you are interested. For our purposes, both of the above lists are useful because they include 'action research'. Third, before moving on to examine more substantial accounts of action research, read and think carefully about the briefer outlines given by writers such as those cited above. Then ask yourself key questions:

1. What do these outlines have in common?
2. What is distinctive (if anything) about each?

Having considered the question 'What is research?', which he defines as 'systematic, critical and self-critical enquiry which aims to contribute to the advancement of knowledge and wisdom', Bassey, (1999, p. 38) moves on to offer a response to the question 'What is educational research?'. Such research, he argues, 'is critical enquiry aimed at informing educational judgements and decisions in order to improve educational action' (p. 39). I shall return to the idea of 'critical enquiry' in Section 2. In the meantime, Bassey's definition, focusing as it does on the improvement of educational action, leads us to the third question 'What is action research?'.

In order to answer this question, we will consider some definitions:

> 'Action research is a process of systematic reflection, enquiry and action carried out by individuals about their own professional practice' (Frost, 2002, p. 25).
> 'Action research is a term used to describe professionals studying their own practice in order to improve it' (GTCW, 2002a, p. 15).
> 'Educational action research is an enquiry which is carried out in order to understand, to evaluate and then to change, in order to improve some educational practice' (Bassey, 1998, p. 93).
> 'Action research combines a substantive act with a research procedure; it is action disciplined by enquiry,

3

a personal attempt at understanding while engaged in a process of improvement and reform' (Hopkins, 2002, p. 42).

'When applied to teaching, [action research] involves gathering and interpreting data to better understand an aspect of teaching and learning and applying the outcomes to improve practice' (GTCW, 2002a, p. 15).

'Action research is a flexible spiral process which allows action (change, improvement) and research (understanding, knowledge) to be achieved at the same time' (Dick, 2002).

'Action research is . . . usually described as cyclic, with action and critical reflection taking place in turn. The reflection is used to review the previous action and plan the next one' (Dick, 1997).

'Action research is . . . an approach which has proved to be particularly attractive to educators because of its practical, problem-solving emphasis . . .' (Bell, 1999, p. 10).

Considering a variety of sources in this way enables us to develop an understanding of action research and its central aims. Before we explore these areas further, you might like to examine the above definitions, identify commonalities and differences, and then write out your own brief response to the question 'What is action research?'. This is an exercise I have given both to undergraduate and postgraduate students. Results usually demonstrate a substantial amount of agreement. Below, I outline the eight quotations once again, together with the responses typically made by practitioners. I have indicated each new idea in bold letters and underlined aspects covered by previous definitions. In this way, it is possible to see quickly both areas of agreement and difference:

'Action research is a **process of systematic reflection, enquiry and action** carried out by **individuals** about their **own professional practice**' (Frost, 2002, p. 25).

'Action research is a **term** used to describe **professionals**

4

studying their <u>own practice</u> in order to **improve** it' (GTCW, 2002a, p. 15).

'Educational action research is an **enquiry** which is **carried out in order to understand, to evaluate and then to change**, in order to <u>improve some educational practice</u>' (Bassey, 1998, p. 93).

'Action research **combines a substantive act with a research procedure**; it is action disciplined by enquiry, <u>a personal attempt at understanding</u> while engaged in <u>a process of improvement</u> and **reform**' (Hopkins, 2002, p. 42).

'When applied to teaching, [action research] **involves gathering and interpreting data** to better <u>understand</u> **an aspect of teaching and learning** and **applying the outcomes** to <u>improve practice</u>' (GTCW, 2002a, p. 15).

'Action research is a **flexible spiral** <u>process</u> which allows <u>action (change, improvement) and research (understanding, knowledge)</u> to be achieved at the same time' (Dick, 2002).

'Action research is . . . usually described as **cyclic**, with <u>action</u> **and critical reflection** taking place in turn. The reflection is used to **review the previous action and plan the next one**' (Dick, 1997).

'Action research is . . . an **approach** which has proved to be particularly attractive to **educators** because of **its practical, problem-solving emphasis** . . .' (Bell, 1999, p. 10).

An examination of these definitions suggests the following:

Action research is referred to variously as a term, process, enquiry, approach, flexible spiral process and as cyclic.

It has a practical, problem-solving emphasis.

It is carried out by individuals, professionals and educators.

It involves research, systematic, critical reflection and action.

It aims to improve educational practice.

Action is undertaken to understand, evaluate and change.

5

Research involves gathering and interpreting data, often on an aspect of teaching and learning.

Critical reflection involves reviewing actions undertaken and planning future actions.

Reading a number of accounts of action research is instructive because, in doing so, it becomes clear that there is both agreement and disagreement among authors as to what are its defining characteristics. For example, Denscombe (1998, pp. 57–8) suggests four such characteristics:

1. its practical nature;
2. its focus on change;
3. the involvement of a cyclical process;
4. its concern with participation.

'Practitioners are the crucial people in the research process. Their participation is active, not passive'. However, Dick (2000) rejects the view that action research 'must be participative, or qualitative or published. It often is and I accept this . . . But . . . I regard its cyclical/ spiral process and its pursuit of both action and research as its defining characteristics'.

What are the consequences of such agreements and disagreements for the researcher? I would like to make two points here. First, if you are undertaking an action research project, it is important to understand that the nature of such work is the subject of keen debate. As we have seen, writers offer their own competing and complementary views as to the fundamental character of action research. Second, if you are completing this project as part of a course of study for an academic qualification, you will need to engage critically with some of the arguments, positions and theoretical perspectives advanced by writers such as those mentioned above. I shall say more about this in Section 3.

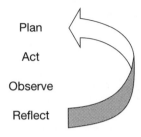

Plan

Act

Observe

Reflect

Figure 1.1   A basic action research model.

Models of action research

In order to illustrate their views, many authors offer diagrammatic representations of action research models. At its most basic, action research can be viewed in terms of the processes outlined in Figure 1.1.

This model has its origins in the work of Kurt Lewin (1946) and has been cited in several contemporary accounts of action research (e.g. Ritchie *et al.*, 2002). From the point of view of teachers and teaching, it involves deciding on a particular focus for research, planning to implement an activity, series of activities, or other interventions, implementing these activities, observing the outcomes, reflecting on what has happened and then planning a further series of activities if necessary.

Dick (2002) has argued that the action research cycle can be characterized by action leading to critical reflection and then perhaps, to further action. As he says: 'So action is followed by critical reflection: What worked? What didn't? What have we learned? How might we do it differently next time?' Furthermore: 'Reflection is followed by action. The understanding achieved, the conclusions drawn, the plans developed . . . These are tested in action.'

The action research cycle is further illustrated in Figure 1.2. Here the idea is to demonstrate that, while action

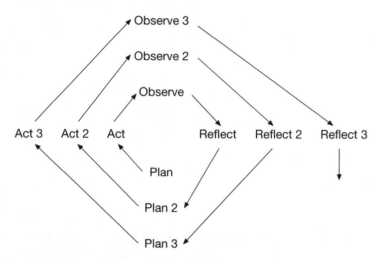

Figure 1.2 An extended action research model.

research can often involve undertaking a single cycle of planning, acting, observing and reflecting, it can also lead to more lengthy and substantial studies within educational settings.

These may be projects that are undertaken as part of study for a research degree, or funded research projects where the timescale and scope of the research extend beyond what is normally possible to teachers conducting small-scale classroom-based research. If you wish to complete an action research thesis for an MPhil. or PhD, a number of general and specific texts will be helpful (see, for example, Cryer, 2000; Dick, 1993, 2000; Phillips and Pugh, 1987; Salmon, 1992).

A more elaborate action research model is offered by Michael Bassey, whose framework consists of eight stages which may be summarized as follow (see Bassey, 1998, pp. 94–5 and Robson, 2002, pp. 217–18):

Stage 1: Defining the enquiry.
Stage 2: Describing the educational situation.

Stage 3: Collecting and analysing evaluative data.
Stage 4: Reviewing the data and looking for contradictions.
Stage 5: Tackling a contradiction by introducing some aspect of change.
Stage 6: Monitoring the change.
Stage 7: Analysing evaluative data concerning the change.
Stage 8: Reviewing the change and deciding what to do next.

The framework is based on three central questions (Bassey, 1998, p. 94): what is happening in this educational situation of ours now? (Stages 1 to 4); what changes are we going to introduce? (Stage 5); what happens when we make the changes? (Stages 6 to 8). To accompany these questions and framework, Bassey offers seven invented examples of possible action research projects. For the purposes of illustration, I shall summarize one of these here. The project focuses on an initial question, which defines the inquiry (Stage 1): 'How do I, as head, know what is going on in classrooms?' (p. 96).

In describing the situation (Stage 2), the headteacher indicates that he has recently been appointed to his post. His predecessor tended to manage the school from his room and visited classrooms infrequently. With the intention of providing educational leadership, the headteacher begins his action research project (Stage 3) by initiating a discussion among the staff and indicating his proposals for responding to the initial question. Over two weeks, he conducts a ten-minute informal interview with each teacher about the question and makes notes which are agreed with the teacher. He writes a brief paper for staff which summarizes the findings and indicates 'a wide range of views from "welcome" to "please keep out"' (p. 96).

The paper is discussed at a staff meeting (Stage 4) and the headteacher attempts to focus on the evident contradiction between his view of his role and the variation of responses made by the staff. At Stage 5, 'Tackle a contradiction by introducing a change', the head indicates his decision to visit classrooms for brief periods, as unobtrusively as possible, to talk with pupils and to look at their work. He says that he will share his thoughts about this process with teachers, on the same day that his visits take place, and he asks them to keep a diary (one brief entry per week) in order to monitor the change (Stage 6).

Another member of staff (possibly the deputy headteacher, although this person is only identified by her initials) offers to read the diaries and to report on staff perceptions of the headteacher's visits (Stage 7). In turn, the head gives his own report about how this process has facilitated his goal of providing appropriate educational leadership. Stage 8 involves reviewing the change and deciding what to do next. This is accomplished at a staff meeting to discuss the reports produced, as a preliminary to agreeing an appropriate course of action.

The final action research model that I shall outline has been produced by Denscombe (1998, p. 60). His framework illustrates the cyclical process in action research and contains five elements: professional practice, critical reflection, research, strategic planning, and action. This model can be represented in several ways and Figure 1.3 outlines one example.

The framework involves beginning with professional practice and reflecting critically on it. Such reflection may lead to the identification of a particular problem or issue that requires research. When this enquiry has been completed, the findings from the research become the starting point for the development of an action plan. Strategic planning leads to instigating change (action), which impacts on professional practice. The cycle then begins again and a further round of critical reflection enables the researcher to evaluate changes made. At this point, conclusions may be drawn and the project may come to an end. However, it is possible that, following the evaluation, some further research may be deemed necessary. If so, the cycle moves on to re-visit this aspect and further 'systematic and rigorous enquiry' (p. 60) is undertaken.

Some authors have argued that one of the major problems with such research concerns the prescriptive nature of its models, as these may restrict the flexibility with which teachers undertake their studies. For example, Hopkins (2002, p. 50) suggests that 'the tight specification of process steps and cycles may trap teachers within a framework which they come to depend on and

1. Professional practice

2. Critical reflection
   (identify problem, or
   evaluate changes)

3. Research
   (systematic and rigorous
   enquiry)

4. Strategic planning
   (translate findings into
   action plan)

5. Action
   (instigate change)

Figure 1.3   A representation of Denscombe's action research model.

11

which will, consequently, inhibit independent action'. Hopkins highlights a further problem when he notes that 'the models may appear daunting and confusing to practitioners' (p. 50).

How are we to respond to this critique? To begin with, it should be acknowledged that some action research models are complex both in their design and theoretical justification. Should this lead to misunderstanding or confusion on the part of practitioners, then these models will have failed to achieve their desired purpose: the improvement of educational practice. This said, I would agree with Bob Dick and others that one of the defining characteristics of action research is its cyclical nature. Essentially it focuses, in turn, on action and critical reflection. While this may be represented in the form of a model (or models), it is important to remember, as we saw in section one, that practitioners are offered a range of possible models from which to choose. The emphasis here is on *choice* and not prescription.

I would agree with those who say that choosing a pre-defined framework within which to conduct a research project is, by its very nature, potentially restrictive. However, rather than this being problematic, it is actually an important indicator of a project's likely success. Research projects should be structured soundly and it must be clear from the initial proposal exactly what is being *excluded* from the work to be undertaken as well as what is included.

To opt for action research must involve intention and critical reasoning on the part of the researcher: it is a deliberate choice of a particular type of enquiry. Once this initial choice has been made, practitioners should then decide which action research framework is likely to enable them to achieve their aims and to complete their studies successfully. This involves either selecting from the range of models available or possibly developing

12

one's own model (on the latter option, see McNiff with Whitehead, 2002, p. 55). To argue that researchers should choose or devise a model of action research within which to shape their studies is not, of course, to advocate the *imposition* of particular models, as these may not be 'representative of the realities practitioners will experience. Practitioners need to see these models for what they are: guidelines for how we hope things will eventually fall out' (McNiff with Whitehead, 2002, p. 52). In order to illustrate the choice that is available to researchers, I shall use Denscombe's model to develop three action research projects in Section 4, below. Having examined the question 'What is action research?', arguments for undertaking it in educational settings will be explored in the next section.

2

Why Undertake Action Research?

Having offered an account of the nature of action research, my aim in this section is to offer a response to the question 'Why undertake action research?'. In order to do this, I shall explore the following key themes: the teacher as reflective practitioner; the teacher as researcher; teaching as a research-based profession; problems with educational research; teacher research and school improvement; and the role of research in teachers' continuing professional development.

Rationales for undertaking action research

The idea that teachers should be 'reflective practitioners' or should engage in 'reflective practice' has gained popularity due, in large part, to the work of Donald Schön. His books on *The Reflective Practitioner: How Professionals Think in Action* (1991a) and *Educating the Reflective Practitioner* (1991b) have a particular relevance for educationalists because of Schön's view that, as practitioners, they should: (1) engage in the study of their own practice; and (2) develop their own educational theories deriving from that practice (see McNiff with Whitehead, 2002). Action research provides an appropriate medium to enable these two aims to be achieved.

This raises the issue of the relationships that exist between educational theory and practice. While I shall return to this theme in Section 3, it is necessary here to make some preliminary comments about it. To begin with, we should note that while educational theory and practice are inextricably linked, the relationship between them has been (and continues to be) the subject of keen debate. Since the 1980s, numerous attacks have been made against the theoretical study of education within initial teacher education and training (ITET) courses. For example, in a pamphlet entitled *Who Teaches the Teachers?*, Anthony O'Hear (1988, p. 26) suggests that 'what is vital in teaching is practical knowledge combined with emotional maturity and not theoretical knowledge at all'. In a subsequent article, O'Hear indicates the limited value which he attaches to the systematic discussion and evaluation of educational theories. He argues (1989, p. 23) that the theoretical study of education 'should be made available to those teachers who feel a need for it' but suggests that it is more appropriate for practitioners to undertake such study once they have benefited from some experience of the classroom.

Dick (2000) explores an interesting aspect of the theory-practice debate when making a distinction between what he calls 'theory-driven' and 'data-driven' research. In order to illustrate the differences between these two approaches, Dick asks two questions of post-graduate researchers. The first concerns whether they wish to engage in 'research that turns first to a body of extant literature and contributes to knowledge by assuming that literature as a given and extending or refining it, or challenging it?' (a theory-driven perspective). Alternatively, do they want to 'deal with the research situation and the people in it as they are, as far as possible putting aside . . . preconceptions', with a view to 'fully experiencing' the context of the research? This is a data-driven approach.

Proponents of theory-driven research would argue that theory necessarily precedes practice and is applied to it. On this view, before practitioners undertaking action research projects can begin their research, they must engage in a substantial amount of reading (about research methodology; the subject matter of the project; the key theoretical issues that underpin the work; research previously undertaken in this field, etc.). Only then, having considered such key issues carefully, can researchers begin their own studies.

However, advocates of a data-driven approach suggest that, in order to undertake research, a greater degree of flexibility is required than is permitted by the theory-driven perspective. For example, it is argued that any prescriptive requirement for researchers to conduct an extensive preliminary review of the literature may lead to them selecting a focus for their work which is restricted by the findings of that review. In turn, this may stifle the potential of researchers to be creative when completing projects, because they may feel the need to remain within the parameters of the research as it was initially conceived, rather than being able to respond more imaginatively and spontaneously as the project progresses. Second, it is suggested that important areas for investigation actually arise from research data collected and that these potential avenues for research might not have been considered by an initial literature review.

Dick (2000) notes that that it is the data-driven approach to action research which is of most interest to him because of its perceived flexibility and responsiveness to the research context. He also makes a distinction between what he calls 'the researcher as technician' and 'the researcher as performing artist'. The former he likens to an apprentice who learns from his supervisor

17

and from the relevant literature how to adopt a particular approach to research.

The second type of researcher is described as someone who undertakes research 'with whatever resources and understanding [he/she] can bring to bear' and who learns from the experience. Dick indicates that these two perspectives involve a shift in the teaching–learning interface and, consequently, in the supervisor–student relationship. He suggests that the conception of the 'researcher as performing artist' involves learning mainly through 'questioning enquiry', in a context where the supervisor acts as a mentor rather than as a teacher.

What are we to make of these two sets of distinctions (theory-driven versus data-driven research and the researcher as technician versus the researcher as performing artist)? I would argue that there is no need to choose between the alternatives offered in either case, as each has its own merits and strengths. Essentially, I would want to ask the following questions: Why can research not be both theory- and data-driven? Why is it not possible to view the researcher as, in some sense, both an apprentice and (at least potentially) a performing artist?

Action research undertaken for an academic award is essentially and inevitably a form of apprenticeship, and success depends on one's ability to do several things with a certain degree of skill. However, as we shall see in the following sections of this book, the competencies and skills required to enable practitioners to complete projects to a high standard can be taught and learned. Furthermore, while technical proficiency is certainly an essential prerequisite for success, this does not preclude critical, reflective enquiry. Indeed, the ability and willingness to ask pertinent questions, to test assumptions, to ask for reasons and evidence to support arguments, and to engage in systematic thinking about relationships between theory and practice, are essential attributes of the researcher (and this irrespective of whether the activities engaged in are conceived of as being theory- or data-driven).

A focus on relationships between theory and practice leads us on to consider the notion of 'the teacher as researcher'. While the idea that teachers should be regarded as researchers, or as practitioner-researchers (see Robson, 2002, Appendix B), is now becoming increasingly popular, several authors point out that this is not a recent idea. Hopkins (2002) offers a concise account of the origins of the teacher research movement, beginning with the work of Lawrence Stenhouse, who directed the Schools Council's Humanities Curriculum Project and authored a number of key publications, including *An Introduction to Curriculum Research and Development* (1975) and 'What counts as research?' (1981).

Substantial contributions to the development of teacher research were also made by John Elliott and Clem Adelman through the Ford Teaching Project, which involved 40 primary and secondary school teachers completing action research projects that focused on classroom-based practice. As Hopkins (2002, pp. 1–2) points out: 'These teachers developed hypotheses about their teaching which could be shared with other teachers and used to enhance their own teaching'. More recent initiatives in advancing the cause of teacher research include the proposal that teaching should move increasingly towards being a research-based profession (Hargreaves, 1996). This would involve practitioners undertaking research activity as an important aspect of their role, with a view to gathering data about a range of issues including strategies for effective learning and teaching.

Rose (2002, p. 45) summarizes some of the key arguments offered by Stenhouse (1981) in the article referred to above. It is interesting to note, over twenty years later, the extent to which these themes are now very much in vogue. Stenhouse suggests that teachers should be at the forefront of educational research and that classrooms provide an ideal context within which to test educational theories. Unless teachers are fully involved in research being undertaken, he argues that they will not wish to be consumers of the findings that emerge from it. Furthermore, teachers have lacked opportunities (other than those offered within higher degree courses) to take on a more substantial role in the research process. Finally, on the traditional view of educational research, practitioners have been asked to justify themselves and their practices to researchers. However, according to Stenhouse, it is researchers who should be offering justifications to practitioners.

In recent years, the nature and purposes of educational research have been the focus of critical scrutiny (see Hillage *et al.*, 1998; Tooley with Darby, 1998; and responses by Atkinson, 1998; Edwards, 1998; Lomax, 1998; and Vulliamy, 1998). Criticisms made of such research, from a variety of resources, include the following (see, for example, Hargreaves, 1996; Rose, 2002). First, there is a widening gulf between researchers and classroom practitioners, and research often fails to focus on 'the real life experiences of most teachers' (Rose, 2002, p. 44). Second, for the most part, research is an activity or series of activities which is done *to* practitioners, rather than *by* them. Third, the findings of research are often written in obscure journals, that are inaccessible to teachers both in terms of the style in which they are written and their location (usually the library of a higher education institution (HEI)). This is inconsistent with a central aim of educational journals: to improve practice in schools and classrooms.

How are we to respond to these criticisms? It seems to me that the best way to do so involves demonstrating the important effects that teacher research in general, and action research in particular, may have both on school improvement and on practitioners' professional development. As regards the first issue, Rob Halsall (1998) outlines the case for teacher research as a strategy for school improvement. Interestingly, the sub-title of his book is *Opening Doors from the Inside* and the volume contains a number of case studies (some written by teachers themselves) that outline the impact of research at whole school, department and classroom levels (see also Carter and Halsall, 1998).

The relationship between research and teachers' professional development is a close one. At the present time, a welcome and much-needed debate is taking place about the nature of continuing professional development (CPD) for teachers and how this might be improved. For example, the General Teaching Council for Wales (GTCW) (2002b), in a document entitled *Continuing Professional Development: An Entitlement for All*, has offered draft advice to the National Assembly for Wales concerning a range of issues.

The GTCW argues that 'all teachers should be entitled to high quality and well-planned CPD provision throughout their career' (para. 19). However, such an entitlement carries with it certain responsibilities: 'to develop oneself professionally and to ensure that professional knowledge and skills are constantly updated' (para. 19). It is noted (para. 14) that: 'CPD activities take many forms. These range from attending courses to school-based learning and undertaking action research'.

Three excellent examples of action research projects to support teachers' CPD are Best Practice Research Scholarships (BPRS) and the Teacher Research Grant Scheme in England, and Teacher Research Scholarships (TRS) in Wales. As regards BPRS, qualified teachers currently serving in schools (including nursery, independent and non-maintained schools) are eligible to apply. It is suggested that they will benefit from the opportunity to:

Enhance their own professional and personal development.
Enable collaborative work with their colleagues to take place.
Raise their own profile among their peers.
(www.teachernet.gov.uk/Professional_Development/opportunities/bprs)

Funding of up to £2500 is awarded to support the development of research projects that focus on classroom practice. As a condition of proposals being accepted, a tutor or mentor must be appointed to assist teachers in completing research projects successfully. Offering some expertise in research methodology, the tutor/mentor is required to make a formal statement indicating how and when he/she will support projects being undertaken, as well as monitor, evaluate and help to disseminate research findings. The above website offers an archive of small-scale research studies undertaken through the BPRS scheme.

For several years, beginning in 1996–7, the Teacher Training Agency awarded grants for classroom-based research under its Teacher Research Grant Scheme. An archive of completed projects is available, containing titles such as the following:

The Role of Handwriting in Raising Achievement;
The Use of 'Diagnostic Probes' to Aid Teaching and Learning in Science;
Developing Skills in Mathematical Explanation;
The Influence of the Head of Department on the Quality of Teaching and Learning;
Developing Individual Education Targets within Whole School Assessment Procedures;
Extending Children's Spelling Strategies;

How Can Primary Schools Encourage Boys to Develop
a More Positive Attitude Towards Learning?;
The Use of ICT in Music Composing;
Teaching Writing in a Foreign Language;
The Teaching of Reading in Years Six and Seven.
(www.canteach.gov.uk/community/research/grant/
index.htm)

The GTCW TRS scheme commenced in 2001–2. Funding of up to £3000 is available to teachers to enable them
to undertake action research projects, supported (as in
BPRS) by a tutor/mentor. Examples of possible research
areas include (GTCW, 2002a, p. 15): raising standards;
introducing new ideas into classroom practice; effective
links and pupil transition between primary and secondary phases; behaviour management and tackling disaffec-
tion; and the use of technology in education.

I have acted as a mentor to two groups of teachers
who received GTCW scholarships. The first group, based
within Wrexham LEA, undertook action research projects in a broad range of areas. The second, also
sponsored by the National Union of Teachers, completed projects on the teaching and learning of thinking
skills in infant and secondary schools. This involved
attendance at two residential seminars, where teachers
were introduced to aspects of research methodology,
issues relating to thinking skills, the development of
research projects, data collection and analysis, and writing research reports.

The GTCW TRS scheme was evaluated in two ways.
First, a comprehensive report was produced by David
Egan and Roy James (2002). This involved the development of an evaluation pro forma for teacher researchers;
a questionnaire concerning the effectiveness of the
scheme, which was sent to their head teachers; a questionnaire for tutors/mentors; and a series of interviews

with teacher researchers, head teachers and line-managers. The report indicated the following benefits to teachers from undertaking action research projects (p. 15): the development of individual needs and skills; motivational and career factors; engagement with good practice; time to develop reflective practice; work-based learning; working collaboratively with other professionals; and learning and teaching gains.

In addition, I undertook my own evaluation of the impact of TRS on enhancing teachers' professional development. Following the evaluation pro forma produced by Egan and James, I asked the following questions:

> How effective do you consider the chosen activity to be in enhancing your professional knowledge, skills and expertise? Please circle your response (1 = very effective; 4 = very ineffective)
>
> 1   2   3   4
>
> How could you further develop the work you have undertaken? Please specify.

All respondents indicated that their chosen activity was 'very effective' in enhancing their knowledge, skills and expertise. Written comments included the following:

> It has made me look at what I do 'day in, day out'. I haven't really been doing anything new, but I have become aware of what I'm doing and have looked at the results of my strategies in the teaching and learning process. I have probably become even more aware of the needs of the pupils I teach and the need to continue to look for new ideas. I have most certainly become more confident in myself and it has given me the 'feel good factor'. I would like to move on . . .
> Time to read and research. Networking and sharing practice. Focus on mentoring: I feel confident to undertake more research. Focus on learning and teaching in general: I have adapted ideas from target groups to other classes.
> The research project has been excellent in enhancing

my professional development, as prior to this I was not even aware of what thinking skills were, let alone being able to implement them in my classroom. It is also an opportunity to undertake research which is directly related to improving teaching and thus learning.
Very effective. The first course produced new ideas. The research process helped me to develop thinking skills strategies and spread them through the Faculty. It improved my skills and those of other teachers within the Faculty.

Responses to the second question included the following:

I would like to have the opportunity to 'spread' my experiences across the school and to work with other teachers within the LEA and further afield. I would like to be supported in doing some further written work (e.g. a teacher's handbook for classroom management).
Adapt my research and findings to other areas of the scheme of work.
I wish to develop further thinking skills strategies within the classroom and perhaps extend to a whole school approach across key stages. It would also be useful to do another research project which could build on the one already undertaken – perhaps to implement thinking skills across the curriculum.
I would like to form a working group within the school to develop thinking skills activities across the curriculum, in order to spread good practice.
I now want to continue my research and spread good practice across the whole school. Thinking skills should be a key area in whole-school curriculum development. I personally would like to initiate this and research my findings.
Develop professional debate among staff to enhance the learning community.

The GTCW (2002b, para. 26) suggests that 'Conditions need to be created . . . to allow [teachers] to be reflective – to learn, develop, and improve as an integral part of their work'. Furthermore, 'There is a need to provide teachers with time to plan, undertake, reflect [on] and disseminate their experiences. This best takes place in environments that foster learning'.

The importance of action research

In order to answer the question 'Why undertake action research?', I have examined several related issues. Considering these together enables us to offer several statements indicating the importance of action research. To begin with, reflective practitioners are concerned with studying their own practice and action research provides an excellent medium for this to take place. Second, action research enables practitioners to explore relationships between educational theory and practice. Third, the critical scrutiny of educational research has led to an increasing emphasis on the importance of practitioners undertaking their own research studies. Fourth, a move towards developing teaching as a research-based profession should lead practitioners to:

1. take an increasingly prominent role in the processes of gathering and analysing research data, and reporting research findings;
2. complete action research projects regularly (and not only as part of higher degree courses).

Finally, action research can have a beneficial impact both on school improvement and on the professional development of teachers. The development of action research projects will be discussed in Section 3.

3

How Do I Develop an Action Research Project?

In order to illustrate the development of an action research project, including data collection and analysis, I shall outline three extended examples in sections 4 and 5 of this book. However, my purpose here is to focus on some general issues concerning: choosing a research topic; developing a research proposal; relationships between educational theory and practice; and the content of research methodology courses or seminars.

Developing an action research project

In focusing on the central question: 'How do I develop an action research project?', you may already have a research topic in mind. If this is not the case, you might like to consider possibilities for research outlined by, for example, Bassey (1998, pp. 96–107) and Macintyre (2000); Wragg (1994, pp. 103–4). As Wragg indicates, there is a wide range of potential research topics. These include:

What teachers and pupils do in classrooms: 'How do they spend their time?'
Classroom talk: 'Who talks to whom about what?'
Classroom management: 'What are the classroom

rules, how are resources, time, space, pupil behaviour, their own teaching strategies managed?'

Pupils' learning: determining the tasks engaged in by pupils, the extent of their involvement in such tasks and degree of success in completing them.

Pupils with special educational needs: the educational experience of very able pupils and those with learning difficulties.

Teachers' professional development: how can they improve their own teaching?

Monitoring and assessment of pupils' work.

Group work: the processes involved in (and educational outcomes arising from) pupils working in groups; the nature of assignments undertaken; decision-making procedures; the extent of collaboration between pupils.

Once you have determined an appropriate subject or context for research, it is necessary to draw up a research proposal. Usually, this will be reviewed by your supervisor (or, in certain circumstances, by a review committee). However, if you are undertaking a funded research project, you will be required to submit a proposal to the funding body.

In preparing an action research proposal for your supervisor, you may be asked to write a brief outline (no more than two or three A4 pages) containing the following information:

your name;
a tentative title for the project (this may be amended in consultation with your supervisor);
the aims of your project;
possible research questions for your project;
the educational setting or context within which your project will be undertaken;

the period of time within which your project will be
undertaken;
the research methodology you propose to use;
anticipated outcomes of your research;
an outline bibliography.

This information will provide a context for your first
meeting with your supervisor. Putting it together in the
way I have suggested will involve you in some preliminary
reflection and research. This is an essential aspect of the
process and a thorough approach at this stage will enable
you to develop a solid foundation for the project as a
whole.

To begin with, you need to undertake a literature
search. The purpose of this is to establish whether the
research topic you are proposing is a viable one. If you
are unable to gain access to a sufficient amount of
reading, both to deepen your understanding of the chosen field of study and to underpin the research you will
undertake, your supervisor or the review committee is
likely to suggest that you choose a more appropriate
topic. Having completed the literature search, you can
begin the process of literature review. This is necessary
because your action research project needs to demonstrate relationships between educational theory and practice, which involves examining critically what authors
have to say about educational issues, and applying the
reasons, evidence, arguments or proof they offer to the
practical context of the classroom, school or other educational setting.

In reviewing the relevant literature (books, chapters in
edited books, journal articles, Internet sources, etc.), an
important aim is to enable you to offer answers to key
questions such as: 'When authors tell me what is happening (or should) happen in, for example, a classroom,
does this coincide with my own experience? If yes, why? If

no, why not? As a result of this review, do I need to introduce appropriate change into my classroom? If yes, how might I do this?'

At your first meeting with your supervisor, you will have an opportunity to: discuss your proposal; indicate why you think it is an important area for research; outline its key aims; and convince the supervisor that you have access both to an appropriate educational setting (e.g. a classroom) and to sufficient theoretical resources (books, journal articles, etc.) to complete the project successfully. During the meeting, your supervisor may suggest some amendments to your proposal or he/she may ask you to give further thought to aspects of it, with a view to finalizing the outline at the next meeting. As a result of these initial meetings, you will produce an agreed strategy for undertaking the project.

At this stage, you may have a number of queries about your research and it is important to make your supervisor aware of these. Never be afraid to ask questions: these are essential to ensuring a successful outcome for your work. There are several reasons why you may be reluctant to ask your supervisor to clarify key issues. First, you may not wish your supervisor (or anyone else) to know that you require additional guidance or support. Second, you may have several questions and do not wish to trouble your supervisor with them. Third, you may not wish to ask questions in front of your fellow practitioners. Fourth, you may be generally unsure both about what is required of you and about how to indicate this uncertainty to your supervisor.

Whatever the reason for such reluctance, you should avail yourself of all opportunities that are provided to meet your supervisor and to articulate any concerns you may have. By doing this, you are much more likely to complete your project successfully. In addition, you may save both yourself and the supervisor a great deal of time in the long-term because regular discussions should lead to fewer errors or misconceptions either in developing or carrying out your research.

If you do not wish to ask questions in front of others, arrange to meet your supervisor to discuss these or see him/her during a seminar break or at the end of a teaching session. Never assume that your questions are so naïve or lacking in complexity that you would be reluctant to ask them. Please remember that your supervisor is as concerned as you are to ensure your success. Eliminating uncertainties at the beginning of a project, or as they arise once it is underway, will do much to accomplish this goal.

The importance of research methodology seminars

In order to enable you to complete your research project, it is usual for HEIs to provide modules or a series of seminars on research methodology. Typically, these focus on topics such as: undertaking a research project; working with your supervisor; choosing an appropriate research methodology; reading for, planning and writing your thesis; citation and referencing; and presenting your research project

I have already outlined some aspects of working with your supervisor. In addition, it is important to attend research methods seminars (if these are provided) and again to ask questions when you are unsure about anything that is being discussed or outlined. When teaching research methodology courses, I begin by offering students a sheet with three headings:

1. Things I know about undertaking the research project.
2. Things I am not sure about in undertaking the research project.

31

3. Things I would like to know about undertaking the research project.

They are invited to write up to five comments under each of these. Then I collate responses and ensure that all aspects mentioned under the latter two headings are discussed. During the final seminar, there is an opportunity for course members to ask any remaining questions and for me to revise key themes as necessary. Issues and questions commonly raised in the first seminar are:

I'm not sure what a research project is.
What are the differences between a project and an assignment?
What is action research?
Am I the only one who feels apprehensive about tackling a research project?
What is the best way to start?
What am I going to focus on?
From whom should I seek help/advice?
How much time will I have with my project supervisor?
Will I be given assistance to get started and have the opportunity to discuss the project on a one-to-one basis?
Will I be supervised so that, if I am in danger of going wrong, I will be told and helped well in advance of the hand-in date?
Can I see completed research projects?
What kinds of question should I be asking?
Is classroom-based research optional, necessary, essential?
Do I have to undertake interviews/questionnaires?
Does every chapter have to have a title?
How should I go about research and incorporate it into my project report?

I am worried about: (1) plagiarism; (2) use of other people's ideas and putting them in my own words.
Use of quotation/citation in the text.
Can we use footnotes or will we use the Harvard system of referencing?
Presentation of the bibliography.
Do I need appendices? Where do I put them in my research report?
Is my project title appropriate? Should the title be a question or a statement?
How should I use my school experience placements/teaching experience in developing my project?
Relationships between educational theory and practice.
How often should I quote?
What should the conclusion contain?
Where do I find information/resources?
Continuity between chapters.
Presentation of the report.
How do I get a good grade?

Your own HEI will provide you with a set of guidelines concerning the completion of the research project. If, having reviewed these guidelines, you have questions about them, or about any of the issues and questions outlined above, please ask your supervisor for clarification.

While you are undertaking your project, your supervisor will wish to meet you, either individually and/or with a small group of other researchers, in order to review your progress. As I have indicated above, attendance at such meetings, whether or not they are compulsory, is also important to your success and allows your supervisor to determine whether you need additional guidance in completing the research. As your work progresses, you may be asked to:

1. submit draft chapters for your supervisor to read and comment on;
2. produce a complete draft of your report before submitting the final version.

Again, although this may be optional, it is important to take advantage of the opportunities that are being offered.

If you are undertaking a funded research project, your proposal to the funding body is likely to have a format which is similar to that outlined by the GTCW (2002a). Applicants for TRS are asked to complete a proposal of between 500 and 700 words which outlines the following: the title of the research project; the aims of the research project; a statement concerning how the research project will help to raise educational standards; the expected outcomes of the research project, both for the researcher and his/her school; the research methodology to be used; the timescale and schedule for the research project, including anticipated milestones; how the research undertaken will be evaluated; and the total funding requested, together with a breakdown of costs to be incurred.

Funding bodies usually require researchers to have academic support in undertaking their projects. This is provided by a mentor from a local education authority, HEI, subject association, or research body, etc. The mentor may assist researchers to develop their initial proposal, as well as offering guidance through regular meetings, workshops, residential seminars, or via email correspondence. Mentors may also agree to read and comment on work in progress, including draft copies of research reports.

Funded projects differ in one important respect from those undertaken as part of a course of study for an academic qualification: they are primarily practical pieces of research. Given this, practitioners are not expected to undertake a formal review of the relevant literature before completing their studies. Nevertheless, some engagement with the literature may be very beneficial, as it is likely to suggest possible topics or themes for research, as well as deepening the researchers' knowledge and understanding of key aspects of the work to be undertaken.

In the next section of this book, I shall discuss a number of possible criticisms that may be made of action research. In attempting to counter these, I shall argue that researchers should endeavour to make their work as rigorous as possible. Examining the relevant literature, even if only briefly, and applying some of the insights derived from it to the context of current or proposed projects, should lead to more rigorous research being completed. This is the best way to respond to those sceptics who are doubtful about the value of small-scale practitioner research.

Before outlining the three action research projects I mentioned at the beginning of this section, I want to return to the list of issues and questions commonly raised by undergraduate and postgraduate students. If you are unsure about what a research project is, guidance will be provided either in research methodology seminars, or by your supervisor. Basically, a research project is a long essay in which you undertake:

1. a critical review of the relevant literature concerning your proposed topic;
2. practical research within a classroom, school or other educational setting.

Projects may vary in length both between academic courses and HEIs.

One difference between a project and an assignment is that the former tends to be a longer piece of work. When

35

faced with writing a research study of several thousand words, it is quite natural to feel some apprehension. However, this can be significantly reduced through attendance at appropriate seminars, by working closely with your supervisor in the ways I have suggested above, and by looking at examples of successfully completed projects.

You should be given opportunities to examine research reports produced by students in previous years. This may be a formal part of a research methodology course, or you may be asked to look at projects in your own time (they may be housed in your HEI's library). This is a valuable exercise as it gives you the opportunity to consider questions such as:

What are appropriate topics and titles for research projects?

What do successful research project reports look like (format, contents, presentation etc.)?

How are chapters or sections of project reports structured?

How do chapters or sections of project reports relate to each other?

Do researchers provide reviews of the relevant literature?

Do researchers justify their choice of research methodology?

How do researchers gather data?

How do researchers analyse data?

How are research project reports presented?

Having produced a proposal and agreed its basic content and structure with your supervisor, you should write a draft chapter (often a review of the literature). The feedback you receive from your supervisor will be useful because it should: confirm whether or not the chapter is of an appropriate standard for success; indicate those aspects of the chapter which are satisfactory or better as they stand; outline those aspects where improvements could be made; detail those aspects which require further work. At this stage, it is advisable to consider carefully the advice that you are given. If you are unsure about any aspect of it, please consult your supervisor. Once you have made appropriate amendments, a second draft should be submitted, together with the first. Sending both versions to your supervisor will enable him/her to see quickly how you have responded to the suggestions made.

Undertaking action research projects: some preliminary considerations

Prior to proceeding with your action research, I suggest that you should:

Undertake reading on research methodology (the bibliography of this book provides a good starting point).
Consult completed research project reports.
Undertake a literature search, enabling confirmation (both to yourself and to your supervisor) that you have access to a sufficient amount of educational theory to underpin your research. Note that a literature search, though not required for small-scale funded research, may be very useful.
Write an outline of your proposed project, including a rationale for it and an account of your suggested research methodology.
Detail the contents of your research project report, either chapter by chapter or section by section (this may be amended during your research).

Having begun your research project, you should:

Meet your supervisor/mentor regularly to discuss your project.
Produce individual draft chapters/sections of the project report for your supervisor to read. This is preferable to submitting several chapters/sections at the same time because, if there are problems with one chapter, it is likely that these will be replicated in other chapters too.
Ensure continuity between chapters or sections of the project report. I shall discuss this further in Section 6.

In the following section, issues concerning the collection of action research data will be explored.

4

How Do I Collect Action Research Data?

Here and in the following section, I shall outline three invented examples of action research projects. In devising these examples, my aim is offer illustrations that demonstrate the following: relationships between educational theory and practice; relationships between quantitative and qualitative research; a variety of approaches to collecting action research data; and rigour in action research.

Collecting action research data: some preliminary considerations

Before undertaking an action research project and collecting data, you should be aware of the main criticisms that have been made of action research as a mode of enquiry (for example, the prescriptive nature of its models, as discussed in Section 1). If you are completing a project as part of a course of study for an academic qualification, you will need to demonstrate your understanding of these criticisms. You will also need to offer suggestions as to how action researchers in general (and you in particular, in the context of your own research) have sought to overcome them. Depending on the nature of your study, it may also be important to explore some problems associated with the practice of educational research in its broadest sense, and these I have discussed in Section 2. Concerns about and criticisms of action research have tended to focus on: ethical concerns associated with undertaking action research projects; rigour in action research; and the generalizability of findings from action research projects. Let us examine each of these in turn.

Denscombe (1998, p. 63) outlines a number of ethical issues that practitioners should consider when undertaking action research projects. He argues that a particular problem facing action researchers concerns the fact that while their projects tend to focus on their own activities, 'it is almost inevitable that the activity of colleagues will also come under the microscope at some stage or other'. This is because practitioners do not work in isolation: 'Their practice and the changes they seek to make can hardly be put in place without some knock-on effect for others who operate close-by in organisational terms' (p. 63) (see also Denscombe, 2002, Chapter 9).

What are the implications of this for researchers? First, they should distinguish between undertaking action research that is personal to themselves and focuses on their own practice, and research that relates to, and impacts on, the work of others. Where the latter is inevitable, 'the usual standards of research ethics must be observed: permissions obtained, confidentiality maintained, identities protected' (Denscombe, 2000, p. 63). Denscombe suggests that practitioners should be open about their research and that they should ensure that those involved in it give informed consent to what is being proposed. In particular, permission should be sought before researchers engage in any form of observation or examine documentation that may have been produced for purposes other than the research project.

Section 6 of this book focuses on the question: 'How do I produce an action research report?' Here, too, as Denscombe acknowledges, ethical considerations are important, since researchers should ensure that any descriptions of others' work or the viewpoints they offer (for example, during interviews) must be agreed with the parties concerned before reports are submitted for examination or publication.

Critics of action research often refer to a perceived lack of rigour in studies undertaken. This is not intended, primarily, as a criticism of individual researchers or of the work they have completed; rather it might be seen as a direct attack on the nature of action research itself. So what are the problems to which critics refer and how might action researchers respond to them? To begin with, it has been suggested (Hopkins, 2002, p. 51) that an overuse of words like 'problem', 'improve', 'needs assessment', etc., 'could give the impression that action research is a deficit model of professional development'. In other words, 'Something is wrong, so do this to make it better'.

I agree with Hopkins that action research offers practitioners a powerful tool to enhance their 'professional confidence' and so, with this in mind, it is important to attempt to speak and write about school-based research as positively as we can. However, Wragg (1994, p. 111) distinguishes between two kinds of action research, which he calls 'rational-reactive' and 'intuitive proactive'. In the first, the researcher examines what is occurring (in a classroom, for example) 'usually with a specific focus on something known to be a problem or in need of improvement, and then draws up a programme to react to what has been discovered'. The second type of action research is undertaken by practitioners who know, 'or think they know, what needs to be done, and so implement an intervention programme first and then visit classrooms to see how well it is progressing' (Wragg, 1994, p. 111). These distinctions are important because they draw attention to different ways of utilizing action research to achieve educational goals. It is often the case that particular problems identified within a classroom or school may be tackled effectively through a sharply-focused research study. However, it is important to remember that this is not the only purpose which action research may serve. As Hopkins (2002, p. 51) indicates, it 'provides teachers with a more appropriate alternative to traditional research designs and one that is, in aspiration at least, emancipatory'.

The notion of a 'traditional research design' is an interesting one, not least because action research has frequently been compared unfavourably to it. In attempting to find out why this is the case and whether such a comparison is justifiable, we need to examine relationships between quantitative and qualitative research. Blaxter *et al.* (1996, p. 60) offer concise explanations of these approaches. They suggest that quantitative research is 'concerned with the collection and analysis of data in numeric form. It tends to emphasise relatively large-scale and representative sets of data'. However, qualitative research 'is concerned with collecting and analysing information in as many forms, chiefly non-numeric, as possible'. The authors note that quantitative research is regarded or represented (mistakenly in their view) as attempting to collect 'facts', while qualitative research aims to explore in great detail 'smaller numbers of instances or examples which are seen as being interesting or illuminating, and aim to achieve "depth" rather than "breadth"'. Although Dick (2000) suggests that action research is often qualitative in nature, it is possible, as we shall see, for practitioners to use both quantitative and qualitative methods in undertaking their research projects. This is a necessary approach because, as Wragg

(1994, p. 9) argues: 'While the counting of events may offer some interesting insights it falls far short of telling the whole story of classroom life'.

Although acknowledging that there is no 'watertight' distinction between these two approaches, Denscombe (1998, pp. 174–6) suggests that quantitative research tends to be associated with: numbers as the unit of analysis; analysis; large-scale studies; a specific focus; researcher detachment; and a pre-determined research design. On the other hand, qualitative research tends to be associated with: words as the unit of analysis; description; small-scale studies; a holistic perspective; researcher involvement; and an emergent research design.

Arguments have been advanced against the rigour of action research on the grounds that: it is primarily qualitative in nature; it is susceptible to 'researcher bias' because practitioners often engage in the study of their own practice; it usually involves undertaking small-scale studies (often of a particular classroom or school); and, given the very limited scope of typical action research projects, results obtained from these studies should not be regarded as generalizable beyond their individual contexts.

How might action researchers respond to these criticisms? The best way to begin is by acknowledging that when undertaking research of any kind, it is important that the results deriving from it are sound. Robson (2002, p. 93) discusses how the trustworthiness of research is usually established. In attempting to convince your audiences (and yourself) that your findings are significant, he suggests that you should ask several questions: 'What is it that makes the study believable and trustworthy? What are the kinds of arguments that you can use? What questions should you ask? What criteria are involved?' In offering answers to these questions, Robson refers to several important concepts that are usually associated with 'traditional' research:

Validity. This is concerned with 'whether the findings are "really" about what they appear to be about' (Robson, 2002, p. 93) or, in Bell's words (1999, p. 104), 'whether an item measures or describes what it is supposed to measure or describe'.

Reliability. This refers to 'the consistency or stability of a measure; for example, if it were to be repeated, would the same result be obtained?' (Robson, 2002, p. 93).

Generalizability. This refers to 'the extent to which the findings of the enquiry are more generally applicable outside the specifics of the situation studied' (Robson, 2002, p. 93).

At this stage, it is important to:

1. determine the extent to which these terms have any applicability to action research;
2. establish how researchers might endeavour to ensure that their studies are as rigorous as possible.

As Robson notes, concepts such as 'validity', 'reliability' and 'generalizability' were initially utilized within the context of traditional 'fixed-design' research, where the aim was to collect quantitative data. Given this, there is a substantial debate as to whether they are applicable to 'flexible-design' research aiming to gather qualitative data (see Chapters 5 and 6 of *Real World Research* (Robson, 2002) for discussions of fixed and flexible designs).

Robson refers to the close relationship that exists between action research and qualitative, flexible-design research, and outlines a number of factors that may lead us plausibly to use the term 'validity' in the context of such investigations. Claiming that a piece of qualitative research 'has validity' is, as Robson (2002, p. 170) rightly suggests, to refer to it as 'being accurate, or correct, or true'. While acknowledging that it is difficult (if not impossible) to verify these characteristics with certainty, he suggests that 'An alternative . . . tack is to focus on the credibility or trustworthiness of the research'. How are these to be determined? Robson refers to a number of strategies for dealing with threats to the validity of a piece of research. These include:

> prolonged involvement in the study (which may take place over weeks or months: 'much longer than is typical in fixed methods research' (Robson, 2002, p. 172);
> triangulation (for example, the use of more than one method of data collection, or more than one observer in the research, or drawing on both quantitative and qualitative approaches);
> negative case analysis ('As you develop theories about what is going on [in your research], you should devote time and attention to searching for instances which will disconfirm your theory' (Robson, 2002, p. 173);
> audit trail (keeping a complete record of your research while carrying it out; this includes raw data such as completed questionnaires, interview transcripts and field notes, audiotapes and videotapes, as well as your research diary or journal – see Robson, 2002, pp. 1–2).

While prolonged involvement in a piece of research may (at least potentially) increase the risk of researcher bias, triangulation, negative case analysis and an effective audit trail may all help to reduce it. Robson also suggests that a researcher's prolonged involvement in a study may help to reduce respondents' bias. This is due to the likely development of a trusting relationship between researcher and respondent, which may decrease the possibility that the latter will provide biased information.

Prolonged involvement, triangulation, negative case

analysis and audit trail are strategies that, if adopted collectively, can reduce substantially possible threats to validity. In this way, the credibility or trustworthiness of the research undertaken is enhanced. In addition, an audit trail offers evidence that you are being careful, systematic and scrupulous about your research. These are important considerations when you are making the case for its reliability.

As regards generalizability, Robson (2002, p. 176) refers to the work of Maxwell (1992, 1996) who distinguishes between 'internal' and 'external' generalizability. These refer respectively to the generalizability of conclusions within and outside the setting being researched. As regards the former, unjustifiable selectivity on the part of researchers (for example, in terms of choosing interviewees, or potential respondents to a questionnaire, or particular contexts for observation research) will substantially increase the possibility that their accounts will exhibit bias.

Robson (2002) points out that some projects may not seek external generalizability. This is commonly the case with small-scale, funded action research studies, as well as those undertaken within the context of most undergraduate and postgraduate courses. Therefore, it is unwarranted to criticize a piece of research in terms of its lack of generalizability when this is neither a stated goal for the work being conducted, nor an explicit intention of the researcher who carries it out. This is not to deny that small-scale action research does not have the potential for generalizability. For example, if researchers share details such as the context of and planning for their studies in their reports, readers can explore the relevance of these aspects to their own research. As Macintyre (2000, p. 66) indicates, 'This makes generalisation a much more serious possibility'. For a discussion of bias, reliability, validity and generalizability, within an action research framework, see Macintyre, 2000, pp. 48–50 and 66).

Dick (1993) details a number of procedures that you may use in order to achieve rigour in your research. These include: using multiple sources when collecting data; continually testing your assumptions; seeking exceptions in cases of apparent agreement and explanations in cases of apparent disagreement; and being willing to challenge your own ideas. As regards the latter three points, please remember that these apply both in the context of your general reading and fieldwork (or practical research).

Examples of action research projects

Examining the above issues carefully enables you to develop a solid foundation for your action research project. In order to illustrate how this might be developed, I shall set out three examples using Denscombe's (1998) action research model. In Section 1, I suggested that this could be represented in several ways and offered one example (see Figure 1.3). I also noted that Hopkins (2002) rightly draws our attention to difficulties which may arise if action research models are offered to practitioners in a prescriptive manner. Given this, I suggest only that the above framework may provide a useful tool with which to undertake an action research project. Its viability will depend entirely on the outcomes of its use within particular settings. Earlier in this section, I also referred to Hopkins' concern about a possible overuse of words such as 'problem', 'improve', etc. With this in mind, I suggest that the word 'problem' in Denscombe's model should be considered as an 'umbrella' term to include the research issue, question, or hypothesis to be examined.

Example 1:   Developing an effective school governing body: an action research project

The research project begins with the premise that an effective governing body is essential to the success of a school. Given this, practitioners may be interested to investigate issues such as: how governors' meetings are managed; the agenda items discussed by governors; the length of time taken up by discussions of individual topics; the level of participation by individual governors, etc. This research might be carried out by, for example, undergraduate or postgraduate students, teachers completing funded research projects; and head teachers wishing to find out whether meetings of their schools' governing bodies are being well managed and whether members are participating as fully as possible.

For the purposes of this example, we shall assume that it is the head teacher of a secondary school, Mrs A, who wishes to undertake the project. She has been in the post for three years and has attended all meetings of her school's governing body (stage 1: professional practice). Although she usually speaks fully concerning all agenda items, Mrs A has become aware that some members rarely participate in discussions. Furthermore, during her informal conversations with governors, many suggested that meetings were too lengthy and that excessive amounts of time were devoted to administrative matters. When asked why their level of participation was low, some made statements such as:

'I am never invited to speak' (student representative).
'I find these meetings rather dull and boring' (councillor).
'I know very little about many of the topics being discussed' (company director).
'Mrs B usually speaks on behalf of both of us' (parent governor).
'I see my role as being to offer support as requested' (staff representative).

Mrs A reflects critically both on her own experience of governors' meetings and the feedback she has received from individual members of the governing body (stage 2: critical reflection). She decides to initiate an action research project with the following aims:

1. To explore the nature and extent of participation in school governors' meetings.
2. To seek the views of members of the governing body about their participation in meetings.
3. To seek the views of members of the governing body about how meetings might be made more effective.
4. To implement change as appropriate (with a view to developing a more effective school governing body).

After consultation with colleagues from her local education authority and HEI, Mrs A agrees to formalize her research by making an application for a Teacher Research Scholarship and receives a grant of £3000. Although not required by the terms of the research to undertake a literature search, she is keen to find out as much information as possible about:

1. school governing bodies;
2. research methodology.

She gains access to her HEI's library database and undertakes several 'key word' searches (e.g. 'school governors'; 'school governing bodies'; 'effective schools'; 'school leadership'; 'educational management') to find important source material (books, journals, Internet websites, etc.). Mrs A then visits the website of the Department for Education and Skills to ascertain whether additional information is available from the School Governors' Centre (www.dfes.gov.uk/governor/index.cfm). She finds a number of interesting publications and then moves on to consider some basic texts on research methodology.

While reading a chapter on 'Observation Studies' in Bells's *Doing Your Research Project: A Guide for First-Time Researchers in Education and Social Science* (1987, p. 95), Mrs A finds an observation chart which offers an account of a school governors' meeting, including agenda topics and the extent of individual governors' participation. She decides to adopt this approach as one means of gathering data for her own research study and invites a lecturer from the local HEI to observe the next meeting of the governing body (stage 3: research).

In order to do this (and following Bell's guidance), the lecturer takes some sheets of lined paper and marks each line as representing one minute. Within a generous vertical margin, agenda items and the starting times for their discussion are indicated. Speakers' initials are written in the margin each time they make a contribution to the meeting. Brief notes about the discussions taking place are included on the sheet and a single line is drawn after each agenda item has been completed. A summary sheet, containing the information obtained from the meeting, is then produced.

Mrs A would like the research project to be as rigorous as possible and so decides to supplement the data gathered from the initial observation. She does this in three ways:

1. repeating the observation;
2. developing a questionnaire which is sent to all members of the governing body;
3. interviewing a smaller sample of the group (stage 3: research).

The research instruments used by Mrs A (observation chart, questionnaire and interview schedule) will be discussed in the next section.

Example 2: Developing questioning in organizations: an action research project

The research project begins with the premise that it is important for professionals working in a broad range of organizations to develop their questioning skills in order to:

1. improve the quality of their own thinking and practice;
2. improve the quality of colleagues' thinking and practice;
3. enhance the learning and performance of individual groups within organizations;
4. enhance the learning and performance of organizations.

Given this, professionals may be interested to ask and find answers to the following questions:

> How often do I ask colleagues questions?
> What sort of questions do I ask?
> What can I do to increase the number, range and quality of my questions?
> What can I do to ensure a greater response to questions from my colleagues?

This research might be carried out by undergraduates, postgraduates, and professionals working in organizations. For the purposes of this example, we shall assume that it is a middle manager, Mr B, who works in a retail business and who wishes to undertake the project as part of his study for an MA in Management. He has been in his post for eight years and has a broad range of experience within his organization. He manages a team of 19 staff. At regular meetings, Mr B requests contributions from the group that focus on work undertaken, progress made, issues and problems that arise, etc. Mr B is keen to explore the role his questioning plays in enhancing the group's learning and development (stage 1: professional practice). Having reflected critically on his questioning (stage 2: critical reflection), Mr B considers himself to be someone who asks his colleagues a broad range of questions. He would like to find out whether his own perceptions of his questioning are confirmed through research and so decides to initiate a project with the following aims:

To ascertain how many questions are asked during a series of meetings covering a range of subjects.
To ascertain the nature of the questioning that takes place.
To ascertain which colleagues respond to questions.
To ascertain which colleagues do not respond to questions.
To implement change, as appropriate (focusing on: 'What can I do to increase the number, range and quality of my questions?' and 'What can I do to ensure a greater response from my colleagues to the questions I ask?').

Mr B gains access to his HEI's library database and undertakes two initial 'key word' searches, 'questioning' and 'asking questions'. These produce some interesting insights and areas for additional key word searches. To begin with, Mr B's discovery of a book entitled *The Art of Asking Questions*, dated 1951, indicates that a concern to improve questioning skills is not a recent development. Given this, he decides to discuss, in one of the early chapters of his dissertation, the historical evolution of questioning in professional settings.

Second, his initial searches lead him to explore topics such as 'reflective questioning'; 'the questioning manager'; 'effective questioning skills'; 'questioning and explaining'; and 'questioning and learning'. Further key word searches in these areas enable Mr B to gain access to a broad range of books, journals, Internet websites, etc. Finally, he undertakes some initial reading on research methodology.

While reading McGill and Beaty's *Action Learning* (2001), Mr B finds a number of references to questions and questioning. He decides to gather research data using two methods (stage 3: research). The first involves a senior colleague observing his questioning during meetings in order to ascertain the number and nature of the questions asked. Mr B devises an observation chart using a category system that focuses on: open questions; closed questions;

affective questions ('How do you feel about . . .?'); probing questions ('What aspects of your behaviour do you
think might be relevant here?'); checking questions
('What you plan to do is . . . Is that right?'); and reflective
questions ('In what way were your colleague's questions
confusing?') (McGill and Beaty, 2001, pp. 128–9). He asks
his colleague to indicate on the data sheet provided how
many questions are asked in each category.

Mr B wishes to be as rigorous as possible in his research.
In order to achieve this, he asks his colleague to observe a
series of meetings, not just a single event. He also requests
not to be given any feedback after each meeting, so as to
ensure that his questioning style remains as consistent as
possible. Mr B supplements the data collected in two ways.
First, he develops a second observation chart. In its initial
form, colleagues' names are written in the left-hand col-
umn. Across the top row, numerals indicate the questions
asked during a particular period. When Mr B asks a
question and receives a response from a colleague, the
observer writes 'x' in the appropriate box. Again, this
chart is used in several meetings. Second, Mr B catalogues
his research by maintaining a personal record of the
process. These field notes detail key aspects of the meetings as seen from Mr B's perspective. The observation
charts developed in this study will be outlined in the next
section.

**Example 3:   Developing thinking skills in the early years
classroom: an action research study**

The research project begins with the premise that young
children should be taught critical thinking, reasoning and
argument skills as part of the formal school curriculum.
Given this, practitioners may be interested to ask and find
answers to the following questions: What are 'thinking
skills'? Do we need to teach thinking skills in schools and,
if so, why? What obstacles exist that may hinder such

teaching? How might thinking skills be developed in schools?

This research might be carried out by, for example, undergraduate or postgraduate students, and teachers completing funded research projects. For the purposes of this example, we shall assume that it is a trainee teacher, Ms C, who wishes to undertake the project during her school experience placement. Having attended a conference on the teaching of thinking skills, which was hosted by her HEI during the previous year, she wishes to gain experience of such teaching as quickly as possible (stage 1: professional practice). Having reflected critically on her last school placement (stage 2: critical reflection), where Ms C was able to teach three lessons with a thinking skills focus, and having already completed some basic reading on this topic, she decides to initiate a project with the following aims:

1. To discuss the nature of 'thinking skills'.
2. To argue that thinking skills should be taught in early childhood education.
3. To outline those factors that may inhibit the teaching of thinking skills in early childhood education.
4. To implement a thinking skills programme with a class of 5–6-year-old pupils.

Ms C gains access to her HEI's library database and undertakes several 'key word' searches based on her earlier reading: 'teaching thinking skills'; 'improving reasoning and argument skills', 'education for citizenship', 'personal, social and moral education', 'critical thinking', and 'the cognitive curriculum'. She finds a broad range of books, journals, Internet websites, etc., and undertakes some initial reading on research methodology.

Having read Costello's *Thinking Skills and Early Childhood Education* (2000), Ms C decides to focus on developing young children's moral thinking, through discussing episodes from *Sesame Street* videotapes with a class of 5–6-year-old pupils. In order to ensure that her research is as rigorous as possible, she chooses to gather data using two methods (stage 3: research). These are:

1. videotaping a lesson taught by her mentor, Mr D;
2. audiotaping two of her lessons and transcribing examples of the dialogues in which she engages with her class.

Ms C wishes to explore the processes of argument that children use when speaking. Accordingly, she amends a model of argument (outlined by Costello (2000, pp. 95–6) and presented in the next section) and analyses both the videotapes and audiotapes with a view to determining the extent to which pupils utilize these processes. Relationships between the collection and analysis of action research data will be examined in Section 5.

5

How Do I Analyse Action Research Data?

I wish to begin by arguing that there is a close relation-ship between the collection of action research data and its analysis. In supporting this view, I would refer to my experience of supervising the projects of students and teachers undertaking a broad range of academic courses, as well as funded research. In all of these cases, prac-titioners engaged in research are busy individuals: project work is only a small part of what they have to do and so there is a need to use time wisely.

How is this to be achieved? When offering research methodology seminars and modules, I refer to a series of related maxims: 'The better the research instruments we develop to collect data, the more reliable those data will be. The more reliable our data, the greater are our chances of undertaking research that merits the label "rigorous". The more rigorous our research, the more likely it is that our conclusions and recommendations will be significant'.

In the last section, I outlined three research projects and suggested methods by which action research data might be collected. It is not possible to examine in any depth, in this limited number of pages, the particular advantages and possible disadvantages of using ques-tionnaires, interviews, observations, etc., within your action research project. However, both Hopkins (2002) and Macintyre (2000) discuss this topic at some length. Also, it should be noted that some authors have devoted entire volumes to discussing themes such as 'developing a questionnaire' (Gillham, 2000a), 'the research interview' (Gillham, 2000b) and 'case study research methods' (Gillham, 2000c). In Section 7, I offer a number of suggestions for further reading that will enable you to examine these individual research methods in some detail.

Analysing research data

My purpose here is to offer some practical examples of data collection instruments utilized in the three projects mentioned previously and to discuss possibilities for data analysis arising from them. Let us begin by looking once again at Example 1, 'Developing an effective school governing body'. As we saw in the previous section, the researcher, Mrs A, collects data by utilizing three research methods: observation, questionnaire and interview. The first observation produces quantitative data (see Figure 5.1) and these are broadly confirmed by a second observation. The observation chart details the agenda items for the meeting of the school's governing body, the number of minutes for which each member speaks on a particular topic, and the total number of minutes for which members speak expressed as a percentage of the whole.

How might this data be analysed? What might Mrs A conclude from it? What is she entitled to conclude from it? You might like to look at Figure 5.1 yourself and then write down your own thoughts on these three questions. Having examined the observation chart, consider the following statements. Do you agree with them? Why or why not?

Evergreen Secondary School
School Governors' Meeting
1 October 2003

	Admin (minutes, etc.)	Curriculum	School inspection	Exams	Discipline	PTA	Staff development	Other	No.	%
Chair (university lecturer)	JHT JHT		JHT III	JHT II	I	I	I	I	29	19.1
Secretary (LEA official)	JHT JHT		III					II	15	9.9
Head teacher	JHT	JHT JHT	JHT JHT	JHT	III	III	JHT	III	44	28.9
Assistant head teacher	III	III	IIII	III				I	14	9.2
Mr P (councillor)		IIII	III		I				8	5.3
Ms L (councillor)			I					I	2	1.3
Mr E (company director)		I	II			I			4	2.6
Mrs R (LEA representative)	JHT		III	II					10	6.6
Mrs C (staff representative)		I	II			I	III		7	4.6
Mr J (student representative)									0	0.0
Mrs B (parent governor)	II	III	II	III	I	JHT		II	18	11.8
Mr Y (parent governor)						I			1	0.7
Total time (in minutes)	35	22	38	20	6	12	9	10	152	100

Figure 5.1 Observation chart.

'Mr J (student representative) did not speak during the meeting.'

'Contributions made by the head teacher and chair-person take up almost half the meeting.'

'Some members contribute very little to the meeting, especially Ms L (councillor), Mr E (company director), Mr Y (parent governor) and Mr J (student representative).'

'The school does not have any problems with pupils' discipline.'

'The school's inspection report was either very good or very poor.'

'The head teacher and assistant head teacher work closely together and are mutually supportive.'

A number of additional statements might be added to the above list and it is instructive to consider exactly what might or might not be concluded justifiably from such an observation chart, as well as what remains an hypothesis to be investigated further. For example, it is unjustifiable to conclude from the chart alone that 'Mr J (student representative) did not speak during the meeting'. As one of my students pointed out:

1. Mr J may have spoken for less than one minute on all agenda items;
2. a concise but effective contribution to a discussion might be (and often is) made in less than one minute.

While collecting quantitative data may make an important contribution to an action research project, it should be remembered that information represented in an observation chart needs to be interpreted in exactly the same way as other data gathered during a research study. The so-called 'facts' that emerge from quantitative research never speak for themselves: they have to be supported by reasons, evidence, and argument. The importance of Figure 5.1 is that it provides us with a number of questions to pursue via other research methods, such as the questionnaire and interview schedule developed by Mrs A. Let us look at each in turn, beginning with the questionnaire (see Figure 5.2).

Mrs A has piloted the questionnaire carefully i.e. she has produced a draft version, circulated it for comment to two colleagues, and then made several amendments as a result of responses received. She is aware of the need to pilot all data-gathering instruments, in order to ascertain the amount of time recipients take to complete them, to ensure that all the questions and accompanying instructions are outlined clearly and to enable items to be removed or amended as necessary (Bell, 1999).

Mrs A aims to collect both quantitative and qualitative data. As regards the former, she provides a variety of possible options for response. In question 2, four alternatives are offered; in question 3, there are five to consider and so on. This reduces the possibility that respondents may reply automatically to questions, or persist in choosing the middle option in a non-reflective manner. On several occasions, Mrs A offers respondents the opportunity to write comments. These will be analysed individually to determine whether common or uncommon themes emerge. In analysing action research data, Macintyre (2000, p. 91) offers a concise explanation of four key terms: themes ('the consistent ideas which emerged'); incidence ('how often something occurred, or the number of questionnaire replies which said the same thing'); patterns ('the timing of the occurrences – whether they were single or in a cluster'); and trends ('the frequency of the patterns'). These enable researchers to offer explanations for what has taken place, rather than just descriptions of events. This schema will be

1. For how many years have you been a member of the school's governing body?

   < 1 year ☐   1 year ☐   2 years ☐

   3 years ☐   4 years ☐   5 years ☐

   > 5 years ☐

2. Which of the following statements best describes your *attendance* at governors' meetings?

   I attend all meetings   ☐

   I attend most meetings   ☐

   I attend some meetings   ☐

   I rarely attend meetings ☐

   Comments -

   -

   -

3. Which of the following statements best describes your *participation* in governors' meetings?

   I always contribute to discussions   ☐

   I often contribute to discussions   ☐

Figure 5.2 Questionnaire.

I sometimes contribute to discussions ☐

I rarely contribute to discussions ☐

I never contribute to discussions ☐

Comments --

----

4. Have you contributed to the discussion of the following topics?

Administrative matters	Yes ☐	No ☐
Curriculum	Yes ☐	No ☐
School inspection	Yes ☐	No ☐
Examinations	Yes ☐	No ☐
Discipline	Yes ☐	No ☐
Parent–Teacher Association	Yes ☐	No ☐
Staff development	Yes ☐	No ☐
Other	Yes ☐	No ☐

    If 'Other', please state topic(s) -------------------

Figure 5.2   Continued

5. Would you like to make a greater contribution to governors' meetings?

    Yes   ☐   No   ☐

6. If 'Yes', please indicate any factors that may inhibit your increasing participation:

    ----

7. How would you describe the management of governors' meetings?

    Excellent   ☐   Good   ☐

    Satisfactory   ☐   Less than adequate   ☐

    Poor   ☐   Don't know   ☐

    Comments ------------------------------------

    ----

8. Do you have any suggestions concerning how governors' meetings might be improved?

    Yes   ☐   No   ☐

Figure 5.2   Continued

Comments -
- -
- -

9. Is the governing body successful in fulfilling its aims?

Very ☐   Quite ☐   Not really ☐

Not at all ☐   Don't know ☐

Comments -
- -
- -

10. Do you have any suggestions concerning how the governing body might become more successful in fulfilling its aims?

Comments -
- -
- -

Figure 5.2 Continued

useful in analysing data that emerges from Mrs A's interview schedule, which contains the following questions:

Why did you become a member of the school's governing body?

Have you found being a member of the governing body a worthwhile experience?

Have you found being a member of the governing body an enjoyable experience?

As a member of the governing body, what would you like it to achieve?

Are you able to attend meetings of the governing body regularly? If not, why not?

How might you contribute to the success of the governing body?

Describe some characteristics of a successful governing body.

Are these characteristics evident in the governing body of which you are a member?

Describe some characteristics of a well-managed governors' meeting.

Are these characteristics evident in the meetings of the governing body that you attend?

Do you leave governors' meetings feeling that you have said everything that you wanted to say? If not, why not?

About which agenda items do you tend to contribute to discussions? Why?

About which agenda items do you tend not to contribute to discussions? Why not?

How, if at all, might you make a greater contribution to governors' meetings?

Could you say something about factors, if any, that may inhibit your making a greater contribution to meetings?

What assistance, if any, do you need in order to make a greater contribution to meetings?

Who might offer you such assistance?

Do you have any views about how, if at all, governors' meetings might be improved?

Do you have any views about how, if at all, the governing body might become more effective?

A model of action research revisited

Having analysed the research data, Mrs A is now able to translate her findings into an action plan (stage 4 of Denscombe's (1998) action research model: strategic planning). For example, this might involve the development of strategies to encourage greater participation in governors' meetings, e.g. asking members to speak on individual agenda items; modifying the agenda to ensure that all governors have at least one topic concerning which they could make a contribution to discussions; introducing seminars to develop governors' knowledge of particular issues, etc. Once these strategies have been implemented (stage 5: action), they will have an impact on professional practice (stage 1) and so the action research cycle begins again. After a period of time, Mrs A engages in further critical reflection to determine the effectiveness of her action (stage 2: evaluate changes). At this point, the research may come to an end, or further research may be required. If the latter is the case, then Mrs A returns to stage 3 of the cycle and engages in another round of systematic and rigorous enquiry.

This format may be repeated in the other two projects outlined in the last section. Before commencing your own action research study, it would be beneficial to revisit the second of the three examples and discuss ways in which stages 4 and 5 of Denscombe's (1998) cycle might be reached. To assist you in this, following are the two observation charts (the first uses a category system; the second is Figure 5.3) that were devised by Mr B during his project on 'Developing questioning in organizations'. How might you analyse the data provided here (given that they are broadly representative of the information collected during the project) to develop an action plan and instigate change within the group?

1. Manager asks open questions   / / / / / / / / /
2. Manager asks closed questions   / / / / / / / / / / / /
                                                 / / / / / / / /
3. Manager asks affective questions / / / / / /
4. Manager asks probing questions / / /
5. Manager asks checking questions / / / / / / / / / / /
                                                 / /
6. Manager asks reflective questions / / /

Finally, we turn to the third research project, undertaken by Ms C, entitled 'Developing thinking skills in the early years classroom'. The following is the amended model of argument she uses when introducing a thinking skills programme to develop young children's moral thinking.

Assessing progress in argument

Processes of argument

The pupil is able to:

express a point clearly;
take a point of view, express an opinion;
make a personal value statement;
express a preference;
give an example;
give several examples;
give appropriate examples;
make a comparison;
give a reason;
give a variety of reasons;
give appropriate reasons;

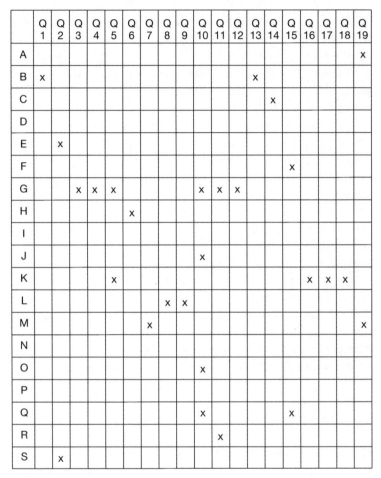

	Q1	Q2	Q3	Q4	Q5	Q6	Q7	Q8	Q9	Q10	Q11	Q12	Q13	Q14	Q15	Q16	Q17	Q18	Q19
A																			x
B	x											x							
C													x						
D																			
E		x																	
F														x					
G			x	x	x					x	x	x							
H						x													
I																			
J										x									
K				x											x	x	x		
L							x	x											
M						x													x
N																			
O										x									
P																			
Q										x				x					
R											x								
S		x																	

Figure 5.3 Observation chart.

quote evidence;
weigh up evidence;
refer to own experience to support arguments;
listen and respond to others' points of view.

Having collected research data by means of audiorecording and videorecording, Ms C now faces the task of analysing it. How is she to proceed? The best way to begin is to examine the videotape of her mentor's lesson and write down the names of children who demonstrate any of the above processes of argument, together with the statement they make and the process that is involved. For example: 'Mary – gives a reason – "Because it would be cruel to animals"'.

This raw data can be transferred to a second sheet, where pupils' contributions or examples of particular processes could be grouped. This will enable Ms C to determine which pupils are demonstrating competence in regard to specific processes. If the argument model was used in a number of different lessons, it would be possible to indicate pupils' progress over time and to alter teaching strategies accordingly. Once Ms C has completed the analysis of the videotape, she can begin to analyse the audiotapes of her two lessons (and perhaps compare her results to those achieved by her mentor). For a fuller account of the processes involved in analysing data from videotapes and pupils' dialogues, see Costello (2000). In addition, Macintyre (2000) discusses a number of strategies for recording research findings.

Concluding comments

In concluding this section, please note the following points regarding data analysis. All the data you collect should be discussed in your project report. If you are unable to analyse all of it, the reasons for your selection of particular data should be made clear. Remember that it is possible to display your results in a variety of ways (e.g. observation charts, pie-charts, bar graphs, etc.). Finally, use appendices to offer the reader a more extensive account of your research than is permitted within individual chapters. For example, if you discuss brief passages from a dialogue with pupils' in the main body of the text, you might wish to provide a more substantial extract in an appendix (see Macintyre, 2000).

I referred in Section 2 to a number of problems that have been raised in the context of educational research. Wragg (1994, p. 101) notes that cynicism about the aims of such research and its impact on practice is evident even among teachers. However, he argues that classroom observation research 'can make a significant contribution to the improvement of teaching competence, especially if teachers and schools, as a matter of policy, research their own practice and act on their findings'.

6

How Do I Produce an Action Research Report?

Once you have collected and analysed your action research data, you are ready to produce a report of your findings. In doing this, it is useful to consider two preliminary questions:

1. For whom are you writing the report?
2. What are the particular requirements or guidelines for writing the report?

If you are undertaking an action research project as part of a course of study for an academic qualification, your audience will include your supervisor and (potentially) an external examiner. Completed projects are usually retained by your HEI, so that they may be read by those undertaking future research projects. Given this, it is important to remember, when writing, that your work will also be read by other practitioners. If you are undertaking funded research (not necessarily for an academic qualification), your audience will include both the funding body and other practitioners.

Requirements and guidelines for writing action research reports

Usually, there are specific requirements or guidelines for writing the action research report. Before beginning to write, consider these carefully. These requirements include a word limit for the project. You may also be given guidelines concerning the presentation of the project report. Here is one example:

Paper size: A4.
Your project must be word-processed using Times or Times New Roman 12 point.
Margins: left-hand – 3 cm; right-hand – 2 cm; top – 3 cm; bottom – 2 cm.
All pages should be numbered.
Use double spacing throughout.
Either spiral ring binding, or soft binding for initial submission and hard binding after examination.

As regards the format of reports, I shall outline examples taken from (1) an undergraduate/postgraduate research project; and (2) funded research projects.

Example 1:   Format for undergraduate/postgraduate research project

Front cover to include title of project/dissertation; candidate's name; degree title; date of submission.
Contents page.
Declaration.
Summary.
Acknowledgements.
Introduction.
Chapters.
Appendices.
Bibliography.

Example 2:   Format for funded research project: TRS

Front cover to include funding body; title of award (e.g. 'Teacher Research Scholarship'); title of project; candidate's name; interim or final report; date of submission.

Summary of the report.

An outline of the aims of the research.

Methodology.

A summary of the results (a complete set of results should be included in the appendices).

Conclusions from the research, including recommendations.

Evaluation of the process.

(See GTCW, 2002a, pp. 15–17.)

Example 3:   Format for funded research project: BPRS

The report is written under the following headings (there is a limit of 500 words per heading):

What were my original aims?

In what ways did I refine my aims?

Research processes I found helpful.

Research processes my pupils found helpful.

The learning points I gained from undertaking the research and what evidence I had to monitor this.

Questions for my future practice.

Questions for my school.

Questions for further research.

How did you disseminate your findings, e.g. within your school, other schools, the LEA, wider?

(See www.teachernet.gov.uk/Professional_Development/ opportunities/bprs/bprssubmit)

As Example 1 indicates, the structures of undergraduate and postgraduate project reports tend to be very similar (and are often identical). The basic differences between the two reports are:

1. the word limit stipulated for each;
2. the levels of critical reflection and analysis required in writing them;
3. the breadth and depth of research being discussed.

Action research reports: a possible format

It is useful to consider the format of a typical report:

Contents page Here you should list chapter and other headings in the order in which they are presented in the report. Remember to include the page number on which chapters, etc., begin.

Declaration A brief statement to indicate the project submitted offers an account of your own independent research. Typically, you may be asked to sign a statement such as: 'I certify that the whole of this work is the result of my individual effort, and that all quotations from books, journals, etc., have been acknowledged'.

Summary A brief synopsis of the project (usually no more than a few hundred words). You should write this once you have completed the rest of the report. The summary draws attention to the key aspects of each of your chapters. You may wish to make reference to your project's aims, its theoretical underpinning, the approach to the research which you have adopted (e.g. action research), research methods used to collect data, results of the research, conclusions and recommendations for future practice; and implications for your own professional development.

Acknowledgements Here you need to thank those people who have assisted you in the completion of your project:

your supervisor or mentor; teachers and pupils, colleagues and other professionals, with whom you have worked; those who responded to your questionnaire or who agreed to be interviewed by you, etc. It is also possible to mention family members or others who have helped you, but please remember that the overall statement should be concise and to the point. Schools, teachers and pupils, organizations and their employees, should not be identified by name, as it is an accepted convention of research that anonymity should be preserved. If you are unsure about this, please consult your supervisor or mentor. A typical sentence might begin: 'I should like to thank the staff and pupils at the primary school where I undertook my research for . . .'.

Introduction Like the summary, this details the key aspects of your project but at greater length. Here, your aim is to outline the nature of the project as a whole. This is followed by a brief, but systematic, examination of the central themes of your individual chapters. You may also wish to refer to the content of your appendices. When writing your report, it is useful to consider it in terms of a 'journey' on which you are embarking. Remember, too, that whomever reads your work (supervisors, mentors, external examiners, or other practitioners) will 'travel' with you in their turn. With this in mind, write the introduction in such a way that it offers an account of the important 'staging posts' of your 'journey': why or how you became interested in the topic being researched; how you developed its precise focus and the project's aims; how your review of the literature developed your knowledge of the topic and influenced your practical research; and how you undertook the research and analysed data emerging from it. Finally, you should refer to the conclusions you draw from your work, as well as possible recommendations for future practice. The implications of the research for your own professional development should also be indicated. Because the introduction should offer an accurate account of your research project, you should write it immediately before the summary (which may be derived from it).

Chapters These constitute the main part of your report. The requirements or guidelines for your project may specify the number of chapters your report should contain (they may even extend to providing you with chapter titles, for example, 'Review of the literature', 'Research context', 'Research methods', etc.). On the other hand, you may simply be asked to set your work out in terms of the reading you have undertaken (which should provide a theoretical underpinning for your study) and the practical research you have completed. In the latter case, it is important for you to develop your own structure for the project and I offer an example of this below. Essentially chapters should provide:

1. a critical review of the relevant literature;
2. information about the nature and context of your research (including methods of data collection and analysis);
3. a discussion of the results of your research;
4. conclusions and recommendations.

Appendices These contain material to which you have referred in the main body of the text, such as blank questionnaires, interview and observation schedules, extended versions of audiotape or videotape transcripts; charts, tables, diagrams, etc.

Bibliography This contains full references to all sources (books, chapters in edited books, journal articles, Internet websites, etc.) to which you have referred in the text (either by means of quotation or citation – see below for a discussion of these). Once again, the requirements or guidelines for your dissertation may indicate a preferred style of presentation for the bibliography. If this is not the case, the bibliography at the end of this book utilizes a format that you may wish to adopt in your own project.

Following is an example of a possible structure for a project report. In developing it, I have chosen the third research project discussed in Sections 4 and 5:

Title

Developing Thinking Skills in the Early Years Classroom: An Action Research Study.

Introduction

Outlines, chapter by chapter, the contents and main arguments/conclusions of the project.

Chapter 1: Preliminary issues to be discussed

Introduction sets out aims and scope of this chapter. Chapter examines important preliminary questions: What are 'thinking skills'? Do we need to teach thinking skills in schools and, if so, why? What obstacles exist that may hinder such teaching (e.g. the problem of indoctrination in schools)? Summary of chapter.

Chapter 2: Critical review of the literature

Introduction sets out aims and scope of this chapter. Chapter offers a critical evaluation of some of the literature on the teaching of thinking skills. Examines the work of selected educators who are prominent in this field. Answers questions such as: are thinking skills being taught in primary schools? How? Is this enough? Summary of chapter.

Chapter 3: The research project

Introduction to the chapter sets out the aims and objectives of your research project: teaching thinking skills to a class of 5–6-year-old pupils. Chapter details the research issue/question/problem/hypothesis to be examined and the timescale for the study. Describes the educational setting for the project, (e.g. school and classroom, etc.). Discusses why action research has been selected as the mode of enquiry or investigation, describes the research tools used (videotaping; audiotaping) and states how you selected and analysed action research data. Summary of chapter.

Chapter 4: Results of the research

Introduction sets out aims and scope of this chapter. Chapter details the results of your research project and examines critically some of the data produced (dialogues with pupils). Results of the research to be explained and evaluated. Summary of chapter.

Chapter 5: Conclusions and recommendations

Introduction sets out aims and scope of this chapter. Chapter outlines a summary of the project, linking results of the research to earlier chapters and offering some conclusions. Recommendations for the improvement of educational practice and implications for the teacher's professional development to be outlined.

Please consider the following points when writing your research report. You should demonstrate continuity and progression throughout the text, so that it reads as a coherent and developing narrative. The best way to do this is to make explicit connections between chapters. For example, Section 1 of this book concludes as follows: 'Having examined the question "What is action research?", arguments for undertaking it in educational settings will be explored in the next section'.

You may be asked to write your report in the first person ('I would argue . . .') or third person ('It is argued . . .'). Sometimes supervisors or mentors have a preference for one of these approaches. Before you begin your report, be sure that you know how your supervisor or mentor would like it to be written.

Remember to avoid plagiarism. According to *Webster's Collegiate Dictionary*, to plagiarize means 'to steal or purloin and pass off as one's own the ideas, words, writings etc. of another'. This may be a deliberate act or undertaken unintentionally. The best way to avoid plagiarism is to ensure that, when quoting from a source such as a book or journal article, you acknowledge the source by using speech marks and providing a full reference in the text. In order to illustrate how this is done, I have provided many examples of quoting from the work of others throughout these pages.

Use both quotation and citation to illustrate your own developing arguments. One way to cite another's work is to summarize it in your own words. Another approach is to refer to particular sources as examples to illustrate the point you are making. For example, you might write as follows: 'I would argue that action research aims to improve professional practice' (Hopkins, 2002; Macintyre, 2000). This is because . . .' Again, I have incorporated examples of citation in this book. I shall return to the issue of quotation and citation in the final section.

Offer an honest account of your research project. Do not attempt to disguise the problems that you may have experienced with it, or the fact that you have been unable (due to circumstances beyond your control) to fulfil all the aims with which you began. For example, it is possible that, having intended for your project to take place over eight weeks, you had to complete it in four weeks. If this is the case, say so in your report and discuss the consequences of the reduced timescale for your research. Did you need to amend your aims? Were there fewer opportunities to collect data? How did you respond to the situation? What data were you able to gather? How did you analyse it? Can you offer conclusions and recommendations on the basis of the work that you were able to complete? Remember that there is no such thing as a 'perfect' research project. All that a supervisor, mentor or external examiner can expect from you is that you have:

1. done your best to think carefully about the development of your project;
2. devised an appropriate project proposal, including a viable set of aims;
3. reviewed the relevant literature as appropriate;
4. attempted to ensure rigour in the research you carry out; and
5. written an accurate account of your work, with appropriate conclusions and recommendations.

Before submitting your report, or portions of it (even in draft form) to your supervisor or mentor, ensure that you have removed spelling, typographical and other errors from the text. Then ask someone else (perhaps a colleague within your institution or another member of your course) to read and comment on it. This will provide additional feedback about your work and increase its potential for rigour.

Finally, retain a paper copy of your report and also keep a copy on a floppy disk and/or on the hard drive of your computer.

7

Recommended Further Reading

As I stated at the beginning, the central purposes of these pages is to enable practitioners to undertake and to offer an account of an action research project. When developing such a project (for example, as part of a course of study for an academic qualification), I suggested that it is important to read widely. This will enable you both to increase your knowledge and understanding of educational theory and practice, and to underpin your research with relevant references to the literature.

While this volume offers a concise introduction to action research, a number of other texts offer important insights into (and sometimes extensive accounts of) its key features. With this in mind, you may find helpful the following suggestions for further reading. Please remember that these are *examples* from what is now a substantial body of written work in this area. It is part of the task of undertaking research that you should reflect critically on source material beyond that suggested by your tutor or supervisor. The texts indicated below will, in turn, offer their own suggestions for further reading.

It is advisable to read some accounts of action research that are located within general texts concerned with undertaking educational or social science research, such as Bell (1999), Bassey (1998), Blaxter *et al.* (1996),

Denscombe (1998), Hopkins (2002), Robson (2002), and Walker (1985). Having considered how action research relates to other forms or types of research, you can then move on to books with a specific action research focus such as Carr and Kemmis (1986), Elliott (1991), Macintyre (2000), McNiff *et al.* (1996), McNiff with Whitehead (2002). The National Primary Trust's *Action Research: A Guide for Teachers* (Ritchie *et al.*, 2002) offers a brief (32 pages) introductory account for practitioners embarking on their own research.

For discussions about:

1. the origins of action research, see Adelman (1993), Elliott (1991), Hopkins (2002), and McNiff with Whitehead (2002);
2. models of action research, see Elliott (1991), Hopkins (2002), McNiff with Whitehead (2002), and Walker (1985);
3. ethical considerations in undertaking action research, see Blaxter *et al.* (1996), Denscombe (2002), Macintyre (2000), McNiff *et al.* (1996), McNiff with Whitehead (2002), Macintyre (2000), Denscombe (2002), and Blaxter *et al.* (1996);
4. criteria for good action research, see Elliott (1995).

Much useful information about action research may be found via the Internet. In particular, Southern Cross University in Australia offers a substantial archive of resource material (see www.scu.edu.au/schools/gcm/ar). Of particular interest to beginning researchers is the collection of papers supporting a fourteen-week introductory course, 'Action Research and Evaluation On Line', and a series of brief comments about action research, 'Occasional Pieces'. If you are proposing to undertake a postgraduate action research project, I suggest you read Dick's (1993) 'You want to do an action research thesis?', which offers guidance on key issues and contains a substantial (and annotated) bibliography.

Within the UK, the Collaborative Action Research Network (CARN), whose website is hosted by the Centre for Applied Research in Education at the University of East Anglia, endeavours to 'encourage and support: action research projects of varying scope (personal, local, national and international), accessible accounts of action research projects, and contributions to the theory and methodology of action research' (see www.uea.ac.uk/care/carn). The website contains information about becoming a member of CARN, as well as details of its newsletters, annual conferences and publications (including the journal *Educational Action Research*).

A number of books offer very useful advice and guidance on the collection and analysis of action research data. In particular, see the following for information concerning:

Quantitative and qualitative research Blaxter *et al.* (1996), Denscombe (1998), Gillham (2000c), Robson (2002) and Wragg (1994).

Questionnaires Bell (1999), Blaxter *et al.* (1996), Denscombe (1998), Gillham (2000a), (2000c), Macintyre (2000), McNiff *et al.* (1996) and Robson (2002).

Interviews Bell (1999), Blaxter *et al.* (1996), Denscombe (1998), Gillham (2000b), (2000c), Macintyre (2000), McNiff *et al.* (1996) and Robson (2002).

Observation studies Bell (1999), Blaxter *et al.* (1996), Denscombe (1998), Gillham (2000c), Macintyre (2000), McNiff *et al.* (1996), Robson (2002) and Wragg (1994).

Audiotape recording/videotape recording Hopkins (2002), Macintyre (2000) McNiff *et al.* (1996) and Wragg (1994).

Diaries and field notes Bell (1999), Hopkins (2002), Macintyre (2000) and McNiff *et al.* (1996).

8

Endnote: The Theory and Practice of Action Research

In conclusion, I would like to offer a rationale for the format I have chosen to adopt in writing this book. Although it is customary to outline this at the beginning of a volume, I have chosen a different approach here. This is for two reasons. First, as I said in Section 1, my main purposes have been to enable you to undertake and to offer an account of an action research project. Given this, my primary emphasis has been on the *practice* of action research, underpinned as necessary by references to educational theory. To offer a substantial rationale at the beginning may have detracted from the essentially practical focus of the text.

The second reason for selecting this approach is that I wanted you to experience each stage of the action research process without having to undertake too much preliminary thinking about its individual stages. I find that this strategy is particularly useful, both for practitioners who are embarking on their first research project and for those who may not have undertaken such work for a number of years. This is because it should help to dispel potential anxieties that would-be researchers may have concerning the nature of the project, the methodologies involved, the theoretical reflection required, etc. Having examined these key issues individually and given some thought to how they might be addressed in the context of your own professional practice, you should now be ready to embark on your project.

To assist you in this, the format of the book is intended to offer guidance at each stage of the process. In thinking about how to begin, I suggest you look again at the six key action research questions. Start by asking yourself: 'What do I understand is meant by "action research"? What are the similarities and differences between different models of action research? Is there a particular model of action research that appeals to me because it would be useful in helping me to structure my project? Could I develop my own model of action research from existing models?'

Now ask yourself the question 'Why should I undertake action research?' and examine the issues discussed in Section 2. Which of these is relevant to your own practice? Do you regard yourself as a 'reflective practitioner' and, if so, why? Should teachers engage in research and should teaching move increasingly towards being a research-based profession? Having considered the problems with educational research that were outlined, how might these be overcome? Finally, what do you consider to be the role of research in bringing about school improvement and in enhancing your own professional development?

As regards your action research project, you need to consider the following questions in the early stages of your work: Have you attended those research methodology seminars that may be provided to support your study? Have you undertaken a thorough literature search and review? Do you have questions to ask before you develop your research proposal? Who might be able to answer these? Having produced the proposal, have you made those amendments suggested by your supervisor or mentor? Have you examined available research reports produced by other researchers?

When you have completed a literature search and gained access to a broad range of source material, you will need to evaluate critically what authors have said about those educational (and other) issues with which you are concerned. In order to do this, you may utilize both quotation and citation in the text. Throughout this book, I have quoted from and cited a number of sources. In doing so, my intention has been:

1. to illustrate relationships between educational theory and practice;
2. to offer practical examples of quotation and citation, so that you can consider how these might be incorporated into your project.

Before attempting to collect and analyse research data, examine again the criticisms of action research that I discussed in Section 4. Having done this, ask yourself a key question: 'How can I ensure that my research is as rigorous as possible?' Before producing your research report, consider carefully both the guidance offered by your own HEI or funding body, and that outlined in Section 6. Finally, in order to increase your understanding of the central themes of this book, it is important to read widely. To this end, I have made a number of suggestions for further reading in Section 7. I wish you success in your research!

References and Further Reading

Adelman, C. (1993) 'Kurt Lewin and the origins of action research', *Educational Action Research*, 1(1), 7–24.

Atkinson, E. (1998) 'Partisan research and the pursuit of truth', *Research Intelligence*, BERA Newsletter No. 66, 18–19.

Bassey, M. (1998) 'Action research for improving educational practice', in Halsall, R. (ed.) *Teacher Research and School Improvement: Opening Doors from the Inside*, Buckingham: Open University Press, pp. 93–108.

Bassey, M. (1999) *Case Study Research in Educational Settings*, Buckingham: Open University Press.

Bell, J. (1987) *Doing Your Research Project: A Guide for First-Time Researchers in Education and Social Science*, Buckingham: Open University Press.

Bell, J. (1999) *Doing Your Research Project: A Guide for First-Time Researchers in Education and Social Science*, 3rd edn, Buckingham: Open University Press.

Blaxter, L., Hughes, C. and Tight, M. (1996) *How to Research*, Buckingham: Open University Press.

Carr, W. and Kemmis, S. (1986) *Becoming Critical: Education, Knowledge and Action Research*, London: Falmer Press.

Carter, K. and Halsall, R. (1998) 'Teacher research for school improvement', in Halsall, R. (ed.) *Teacher Research and School Improvement: Opening Doors from the*

Inside, Buckingham: Open University Press, pp. 71–90.

Costello, P. J. M. (2000) *Thinking Skills and Early Childhood Education,* London: David Fulton Publishers.

Cryer, P. (2000) *The Research Student's Guide to Success,* 2nd edn, Buckingham: Open University Press.

Denscombe, M. (1998) *The Good Research Guide for Small-Scale Social Research Projects,* Buckingham: Open University Press.

Denscombe, M. (2002) *Ground Rules for Good Research: A Ten Point Guide for Social Researchers,* Buckingham: Open University Press.

Dick, B. (1993) 'You want to do an action research thesis?', www.scu.edu.au/schools/gcm/ar/art/arthesis.html

Dick, B. (1997) 'Action learning and action research', www.scu.edu.au/schools/gcm/ar/arp/actlearn.html

Dick, B. (2000) 'Postgraduate programmes using action research', www.scu.edu.au/schools/gcm/ar/arp/ppar.html

Dick, B. (2002) 'Action research: action *and* research', www.scu.edu.au/schools/gcm/ar/arp/aandr.html

Edwards, A. (1998) 'A careful review but some lost opportunities', *Research Intelligence,* BERA Newsletter No. 66, pp. 15–16.

Egan, D. and James, R. (2002) *An Evaluation for the General Teaching Council for Wales of the Professional Development Pilot Projects 2001–2002,* Bristol: PPI Group.

Elliott, J. (1991) *Action Research for Educational Change,* Buckingham: Open University Press.

Elliott, J. (1995) 'What is good action research? – some criteria', *Action Researcher,* 2, 10–11.

Frost, P. (2002) 'Principles of the action research cycle', in Ritchie, R., Pollard, A., Frost, P. and Eaude, T. (eds) *Action Research: A Guide for Teachers. Burning Issues in*

Primary Education, Issue No. 3, Birmingham: National Primary Trust, pp. 24–32.

General Teaching Council for Wales (GTCW) (2002a) *Professional Development Pilot Projects: Information Booklet 2002–2003,* Cardiff: GTCW.

General Teaching Council for Wales (GTCW) (2002b) *Continuing Professional Development: An Entitlement for All,* Cardiff: GTCW.

Gillham, B. (2000a) *Developing a Questionnaire,* London: Continuum.

Gillham, B. (2000b) *The Research Interview,* London: Continuum.

Gillham, B. (2000c) *Case Study Research Methods,* London: Continuum.

Halsall, R. (ed.) (1998) *Teacher Research and School Improvement: Opening Doors from the Inside,* Buckingham: Open University Press.

Hargreaves, D. (1996) 'Teaching as a research-based profession: possibilities and prospects', Teacher Training Agency Annual Lecture, April.

Hillage, J., Pearson, R., Anderson, A. and Tamkin, P. (1998) *Excellence in Research on Schools.* Research Report No. 74, Norwich: Her Majesty's Stationery Office.

Hopkins, D. (2002) *A Teacher's Guide to Classroom Research,* 3rd edn, Buckingham: Open University Press.

Lewin, K. (1946) 'Action research and minority problems', *Journal of Social Issues,* 2, 34–46.

Lomax, P. (1998) 'Researching the researchers', *Research Intelligence,* BERA Newsletter No. 66, 13–15.

McGill, I. and Beaty, L. (2001) *Action Learning: A Guide for Professional, Management and Educational Development,* London: Kogan Page.

Macintyre, C. (2000) *The Art of Action Research in the Classroom,* London: David Fulton Publishers.

McNiff, J., Lomax, P. and Whitehead, J. (1996) *You and Your Action Research Project,* London: RoutledgeFalmer.

McNiff, J. with **Whitehead, J.** (2002) *Action Research: Principles and Practice*, 2nd edn, London: RoutledgeFalmer.

Maxwell, J. A. (1992) 'Understanding and validity in qualitative research', *Harvard Educational Review*, 62, 279–300.

Maxwell, J. A. (1996) *Qualitative Research Design: An Interactive Approach*, California: Sage.

O'Hear, A. (1988) *Who Teaches the Teachers?*, London: The Social Affairs Unit.

O'Hear, A. (1989) 'Teachers can become qualified in practice', *The Guardian*, 24 January, p. 23.

Payne, S. L. (1951) *The Art of Asking Questions*, Princeton: Princeton University Press.

Phillips, E. M. and **Pugh, D. S.** (1987) *How to Get a Ph.D.: A Handbook for Students and Their Supervisors*, Buckingham: Open University Press.

Ritchie, R., Pollard, A., Frost, P. and **Eaude, T.** (2002) *Action Research: A Guide for Teachers. Burning Issues in Primary Education*, No. 3, Birmingham: National Primary Trust.

Robson, C. (2002) *Real World Research*, 2nd edn, Oxford: Blackwell.

Rose, R. (2002) 'Teaching as a "research-based profession": encouraging practitioner research in special education', *British Journal of Special Education*, 29(1), 44–8.

Salmon, P. (1992) *Achieving a Ph.D.: Ten Students' Experience*, Stoke-on-Trent: Trentham Books.

Schön, D. A. (1991a) *The Reflective Practitioner: How Professionals Think in Action*, Aldershot: Avebury.

Schön, D. A. (1991b) *Educating the Reflective Practitioner*, San Francisco: Jossey-Bass Publishers.

Stenhouse, L. (1975) *An Introduction to Curriculum Research and Development*, London: Heinemann.

Stenhouse, L. (1981) 'What counts as research?', *British Journal of Educational Studies,* 29(2), 103–14.

Tooley, J. with Darby, D. (1998) *Educational Research: A Critique,* London: Office for Standards in Education.

Vulliamy, D. (1998) 'A complete misunderstanding of our position . . . trivialises our arguments', *Research Intelligence,* BERA Newsletter No. 66, pp. 17–18.

Walker, R. (1985) *Doing Research: A Handbook for Teachers,* London: Routledge.

Wragg, E. C. (1994) *An Introduction to Classroom Observation,* London: Routledge.

Index